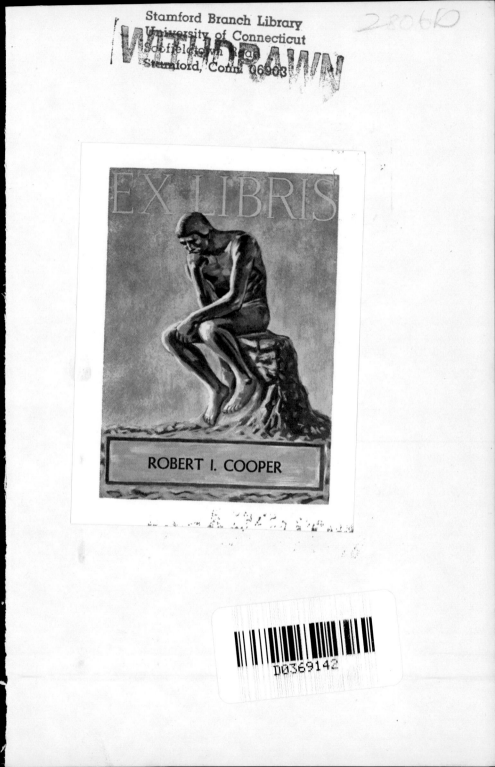

WOODROW WILSON

Also by Arthur S. Link

The Papers of Woodrow Wilson, 3 volumes to date (Editor-in-Chief)

Wilson, 5 volumes to date

Woodrow Wilson and the Progressive Era, 1910–1917

Wilson the Diplomatist

Woodrow Wilson, A Brief Biography

American Epoch, A History of the United States Since the 1890's

The Growth of American Democracy

Woodrow Wilson

A PROFILE

EDITED BY

ARTHUR S. LINK

AMERICAN PROFILES

General Editor: Aïda DiPace Donald

American Century Series
HILL AND WANG : NEW YORK

Copyright © 1968 by Arthur S. Link
All rights reserved
Library of Congress catalog card number: 68–14783

First edition May 1968
Second printing September 1968

Manufactured in the United States of America

Contents

10/75

Introduction

IN SEARCH OF
WOODROW WILSON'S PERSONALITY

It is by no means impossible for a diligent researcher to discover the public facts about most important individuals, but it is always extraordinarily difficult to get behind the façade and to study, describe, and re-create verbally the personality of a subject. It requires several years of intense analysis for a psychiatrist to probe into the psyche of a live subject. How much more difficult it is for the scholar who has to rely only upon the written word!

Ordinary difficulties aside, it is little wonder that the personality of Woodrow Wilson has so long remained a mystery or been only imperfectly understood. Ray Stannard Baker, Wilson's authorized biographer, was originally partially responsible for the mystification. Baker had exclusive possession of what were thought to be the entire body of the Wilson Papers until he completed his biography in the late 1930's. His eight-volume *Woodrow Wilson: Life and Letters* (1927–1939) was for many years the only full-scale biography available. Indispensable though it was, Baker's work embodied a portrait of the Wilsonian personality that was something of a caricature.

Baker labored under some obvious handicaps. First, his long acquaintance with and intense admiration of Wilson not only influenced him in obvious ways but also profoundly affected his reading of the documentary evidence. Second, Baker *was* writing the authorized biography, and writing it under Mrs. Wilson's watchful eye. Third, Baker, because of his own limitations, was never fully sensitive to the subtleties and changes in Wilson's religious thought and their manifestations in Wilson's personal and public conduct. Finally, as Robert Bannister's acute study *Ray Stannard Baker: The Mind and Thought of a Progressive* has recently shown, Baker to a large degree imposed his own personality profile upon Wilson.

Whatever the cause, the result was a portrait that was scarcely credible to critical readers. The Wilson of the Baker biography is too good to be true—or human. By robbing Wilson of his humanity, Baker unconsciously created a less interesting as well as a less credible character. For example, Baker was so intent upon protecting Wilson's reputation against contemporary slanderers that he ended by portraying his subject as being mainly feminine in personality, if not virtually a sexual neuter. Perhaps this statement is too strong. In any event, Baker refused either to come to grips with or to describe the strong masculine drive that was one of the great sources of Wilson's life power.

It was very difficult for biographers to get a clear view of the Wilsonian personality for years after the completion of Baker's biography simply because the essential biographical materials were either missing or unavailable. Such absolutely indispensable collections as the letters between Wilson and his first and second wives, Ellen Axson Wilson and Edith Bolling Wilson, and Wilson's letters to his friend and intimate correspondent, Mary Allen Hulbert, were closed to all scholars until the 1960's. Even worse, the great body of the Wilson Papers for the first forty years of Wilson's life were hidden in trunks in the Wilson house on S Street in Washington. Only after the discovery of this collection was it possible, for example, to understand the relationship between Wilson and his father, the Reverend Dr. Joseph Ruggles Wilson. Enough was known for all biographers to affirm that this relationship was indubitably the most important force during the formative years of Woodrow Wilson's life. And yet all biographers, Baker included, had never seen the relationship with anything but very imperfect and distorted vision.

Biographers and historians in pursuit of truth necessarily have to use whatever evidence is at hand. In Wilson's case, the unavailability of the most elementary personal documents forced historians and biographers to rely heavily upon the letters, diaries, etc., of his contemporaries. These sources are of course indispensable: without them, we could never see many facets of Wilson's personality. However, the light from these sources is distorted by the prisms of the contemporary's own prejudices, varying ability to understand personality, and above all his purpose in writing a letter, memorandum, or diary entry. There is distortion both ways, to be sure. Contemporaries who ardently admired Wilson tended to leave documentary evidence just as distorted as that left by individuals who had strong feelings against Wilson.

There are numerous examples of the dangers of relying too much on the testimony left by Wilson's close associates. One such example among the serious works is a psychological study of Wilson by Alexander L. and Juliette L. George, *Woodrow Wilson and Colonel House,* published in 1956. This study, like many others of the Wilson era, is based heavily on the diary of Colonel Edward M. House, Wilson's intimate adviser. This massive diary is one of the most important sources of Wilsonian biography. Yet we are only now beginning to see the degree to which Colonel House wrote for the specific purpose of creating his own version of the historical record. Portions of the House diary are simply unreliable, and the truth about any particular episode can be determined only when one is able to compare House's account with

accounts left by other participants. It is more important to say that
House's numerous comments on Wilson's actions and personality
have to be read in light of House's unrelenting effort to defend,
through his diary, the superiority of his own mind, intellect, and
policies against Wilson's.

One has to be equally careful in using the various memoranda
left by Wilson's Secretary of State from 1915 to 1920, Robert
Lansing—the papers usually referred to as the Lansing diary. I
quoted one of these memoranda—a personality profile—at length
in my *Wilson: The New Freedom* (1956). Were I rewriting that
book, I would probably use the extract again. But I would be
careful to point out that it was the testimony of a bitter man, and
that the bitterness that Lansing felt was not by any means justified
by Wilson's treatment of his Secretary of State.

Is it possible really to know Woodrow Wilson? And is it
possible to construct a full and accurate profile of his personality?

One has to begin the answer to the first question by saying that
many of the major contours of Wilson's personality have been long
known and written about. Virtually all contemporaries and historical writers, friendly and hostile, have agreed that Wilson was
different from the run of ordinary men. His personality was, in
short, strong, aggressive, dominant, and, to many persons, compelling. He had the power to command loyalty, to charm, and also
to repel. The testimony of his contemporaries, from his student
days to the end of his life, is so unanimous on this point as to be
conclusive.

In addition, all observers, contemporary and historical, agree
that Wilson was an extraordinarily intense person. He was not
merely a well-disciplined and hard worker, but a person who was
always driving, never satisfied with momentary achievements and
triumphs. Psychologists have attributed this inner drive to Wilson's
highly developed superego, derived particularly from the demands
and expectations of his father.

The great majority of Wilson's contemporaries also agree that he had a first-class mind, though one more adept at synthesizing ideas than originating them. He was, as Gamaliel Bradford, Jr., put it, a "creature of brains." But, as Bradford and other writers have made clear, Wilson was interested in ideas for the practical use to which they might be put, and hardly at all in abstract speculation.

All observers strongly affirm that Wilson was an idealist, and all his close friends agree that he had a strong conscience, a highly developed ethical system, and deep Christian faith. However, very few of Wilson's contemporaries understood the nature of Wilson's idealism, and some secondary writers have followed them in incorrectly interpreting it as being largely moralism and slavish obedience to an ethical system. Recent research has put this whole matter in a new perspective. Wilson, at least in his mature years, was not, technically, an idealist, even though he continued to use the language of idealism. On the contrary, he had little use for ethical abstractions or ideals as these terms have been defined by philosophers. Having discovered the meaning of justification by faith in about 1905 and 1906, Wilson became increasingly afterward a Christian realist whose ethics were very much affected by the context and circumstances of any particular situation demanding a moral decision.

Most contemporaries and biographers also agree that Wilson was by nature headstrong, opinionated, and combative. Some critics have asserted that he had no capacity for self-criticism or understanding, would brook no opposition, and cut off friends who disagreed with him.

Finally, views of Wilson the man in day-to-day relationships have varied according to the subjective reactions of contemporaries and biographers. To persons who did not like him, Wilson seemed cold, even capable of some personal cruelty. To members of his family and to his friends, on the other hand, Wilson was outgoing, warmhearted, and generously capable of friendship.

The foregoing generalizations summarize a fairly extensive and intimate understanding of Wilson's personality—a much better understanding, indeed, than we possess about most historic personages. Is it possible to know Wilson even better? Is it possible to define sharply what is now described imprecisely in talking about various aspects of his personality? Can we probe behind the façade of behavior to the wellsprings of motivation? Or is what Wilson once said about Lincoln also true of himself? "That brooding spirit had no real familiars. I get the impression that it never spoke out in complete self-revelation, and that it could not reveal itself completely to anyone."

Wilson was not describing himself. We are now in a position to know him better than probably any other important individual in history. We are in a position to know him better than any of his contemporaries did, even members of his family. We can now probably know him better than he knew himself.

From his student days onward, Wilson wrote constantly—in letters, lectures, articles, editorials, essays, and diaries. He never held anything back because he was incapable of successful dissimulation. He poured out his thoughts in torrents of words. The form did not particularly matter. To be sure, he expressed himself more fully and frankly in diaries and in letters to members of his family and to intimate friends. As he once put it in a letter, "I am apt to let my thoughts and feelings slip more readily from the end of my pen than from the end of my tongue." He revealed himself differently but perhaps just as importantly in essays in literary criticism, lectures on the Reformation, diplomatic notes, sermons, and political speeches.

Wilson rarely threw anything away. He saved not only letters and the things that one usually finds in personal papers, but also thousands of envelopes, loose pages, scraps of paper, etc., as well as his books. On many of these he jotted down thoughts as they came from his mind. Even though he did not usually keep copies of his personal letters, many of his correspondents did save them, and it has been possible to reconstruct virtually a complete Wilsonian archive.

The present writer and his colleagues at Princeton University are now deep into this vast collection, and the early fruits of their work, the first three volumes of *The Papers of Woodrow Wilson,* are in print. In addition, four other volumes in various stages of production cover Wilson's life to 1893.

It would require a fairly sizable volume adequately to relate what the documents in these first volumes of *The Papers* tell us about the formation and maturing of Wilson's personality. One can say in summary that it is evident that:

1. The relationship between Wilson and his father was very determinative. The letters show plainly enough why Wilson later called his father "the best instructor, the most inspiring companion . . . that a youngster ever had." The relationship during its early stages was of course that of father and son, master and pupil. Dr. Wilson had exacting standards and gave the most extraordinary attention to his son's intellectual and literary development. However the extant letters indicate very strongly that Dr. Wilson was more intent upon drawing out his son's own talent than upon imposing ideas and techniques upon him, and that he evoked these talents with measured encouragement and love. This relationship was, actually, liberating and creative for both partners. It had become a relationship between equals by the time of Woodrow Wilson's maturity, and from this time forward the father increasingly drew strength and ideas from his son.

2. Wilson's Mother, Janet Woodrow Wilson, was in her own quiet way a much greater influence upon her son than we had ever known. Indeed, it is clear that Wilson derived his ideal of womanhood in large measure from the example set by his mother.

3. Dr. and Mrs. Wilson were proud, sensitive, and quick to resent alleged slights. Midwesterners who had moved to the South before the Civil War, they had warmly embraced the Southern

cause. Even so, they were obviously never fully accepted by the
extremists called "Southrons" and "unreconstructed rebels," and
this antagonism, if not hostility, accentuated the Wilsons' sensitivity and caused them to find self-protection in family clannish-
ness and pride. Woodrow Wilson came by his own pride and
sensitivity quite naturally.

4. Wilson was a precocious child. Family tradition had it that he
was a slow starter—this tradition says, for example, that he did
not learn to read until he was nine. This may or may not be
correct. But Wilson learned rapidly enough once he began, and by
his eighteenth year he had acquired the fundamental habits of hard
work and incredible self-discipline that were to characterize everything that he did from his undergraduate days at Princeton onward.

5. Wilson's education in ancient history and ancient and modern languages, modern history, political science, economics, legal
studies, and literature was much more extensive and profound than
we had ever imagined. To be sure, much of his undergraduate
education was self-motivated and self-acquired, and this fact is
another early evidence of his iron self-discipline. But at The Johns
Hopkins University he acquired what was probably as good an
education in the social sciences as it was possible to acquire at the
time, the 1880's.

6. During the formative years of his life, Wilson had a keen
capacity for self-criticism and seems to have suffered from insecurity on account of his inability to achieve as rapidly as he
thought he should. However, he seems to have come to full self-
realization—and to terms with himself, at least temporarily—by
1890. Wilson's self-realization. incidentally, did not do full justice
to his intellectual powers.

7. Normal insecurity during his early years drove Wilson to
depend upon the love of his family and friends, but he also clearly
developed a high capacity for wholehearted friendship. His own

numerous comments about his inability to give himself in friendship are to be taken with some large grains of salt.

8. Wilson was from his youth onward, as I have said, extraordinarily intense; that is to say, he worked with unrelenting efforts to achieve his self-appointed goals. His superego undoubtedly set these goals, but power came from his own life force, and one can only conclude that the genes combined with family influences and environment to make him what he was.

9. The incidence and intensity of Wilson's psychosomatic illnesses during these formative years have been much exaggerated by Baker, and particularly by Sigmund Freud and William C. Bullitt in their *Thomas Woodrow Wilson, A Psychological Study* (1967). Ironically, insufficient attention has been paid to the exact nature and effects of Wilson's strokes in 1906 and 1919. Edwin A. Weinstein, M.D., of the Washington School of Psychiatry, has begun what promises to be a thorough investigation. His tentative conclusions to date are that Wilson suffered a severe stroke with accompanying brain damage in 1906, that he achieved substantial and almost miraculous recovery through sheer determination, and that he suffered a massive stroke with considerable damage to the brain in 1919. We know that subtle but very important changes occurred in Wilson's personality in 1906; that, for example, he became less tractable than he had been before and more intense than ever in pursuing goals. It seems likely that Wilson's almost self-destructive behavior during the controversies at Princeton from 1907 to 1910 and over ratification of the Treaty of Versailles from 1919 to 1920 was profoundly if not decisively influenced by certain brain damage. But we will not be able to speak authoritatively on this matter until Dr. Weinstein and other medical experts have completed their work.

10. His personal advantages and precocity aside, Wilson seems to have been a remarkably normal person during the first forty years of his life. His childhood was serene in spite of growing up in the

South during the Civil War and Reconstruction. He may or may not have been robust as a boy—we simply have no good evidence on this point—but he knew most of the pleasures of boyhood. He played baseball, and football to a lesser degree, and maintained an avid interest in sports. He dreamed of building great warships and of commanding large armies in the field. Like most boys from the same kind of families in the Victorian era, he was something of a prig, at least by our own standards. He fell deeply in love and knew all the joys of romance and courtship. He had numerous male friends.

Students of personality, and particularly of Wilson's personality, will be able to make their own analyses and form their own conclusions as the evidence becomes available in *The Papers of Woodrow Wilson*. Indeed, we will soon have the evidence in print for a detailed study of Wilson's mature personality.

My main objective in assembling this little book has been to introduce readers to Woodrow Wilson the man. The personal literature on Wilson is immense, and my only difficulty has been in choosing from among a large number of excellent pieces, all of which would have served my purpose equally well. Since this book was never meant to be a substitute for a biography, I felt no compulsion to see that every aspect of Wilson's life was covered. However, the plethora of good materials made it possible to put together a collection that affords both partial chronological coverage and, at the end, some historical perspective on Wilson's contributions to modern history.

The opening selection from William Bayard Hale's campaign biography, written in 1912, remains the single best source for Wilson's childhood, as it was based largely upon Wilson's own reminiscences. Archibald W. Patterson's memoir of Wilson at the University of Virginia is well researched and objective. Unfortunately, we have no comparable studies of Wilson as a student at Davidson, Princeton, or Johns Hopkins. Wilson was a full-time teacher for seventeen years and a part-time teacher for eight additional years, and reminiscences by former students and colleagues abound. Carl F. Price's study of Wilson at Wesleyan and Bliss Perry's of Wilson at Princeton stand out for accuracy, insight, and descriptive detail. William Starr Myers' memoir of Wilson as president of Princeton is notable for its objectivity and appreciation of Wilson's great contributions to the university.

We have a large number of personality profiles of Wilson after he entered politics in 1910. The best were written by contemporaries, mainly by reporters whose work made the period 1900 to 1920 the golden age of American journalism. Burton J. Hendrick's essay on Wilson as Governor of New Jersey remains the finest single brief study of this subject. Flawed by adulation though it is, this article illuminates the thought and actions of the burgeoning statesman as no other single piece has ever done. Dr. Grayson's modest but moving pen portrait introduces us to Wilson the President as a human being, while William Bayard Hale's article reveals a President just becoming accustomed to daily routine in the White House. In the following three selections, Wilson talks, directly and through reporters, about himself, his views of Presidential leadership, and the burdens of his office. It is, incidentally, no accident that Wilson's words have a very familiar ring to our own ears, for he was the first President of the United States to carry the burdens of playing a decisive role in world affairs, and he carried these burdens virtually alone, without the assistance of the huge executive apparatus that we know today. The agony of such responsibility has never been more poignantly voiced than in Frank Cobb's reminiscence of his talk with Wilson just when the President was moving toward the decision for war in 1917.

The literature on the war, the Paris Peace Conference, and Wilson in retirement is so voluminous that one could easily edit a volume of this kind on each subject, and what I have selected might seem very inadequate indeed to some readers. Ray Stannard Baker's portrait of Wilson in Paris gives at least a glimpse of the man during this momentous conference, while James Kerney's account of conversations with Wilson just before his death provides a fitting conclusion to the biographical selections.

Personality, particularly Wilson's personality, is a fascinating study in itself, and I hope that these selections have made Woodrow Wilson live again. But Wilson was not only an intriguing human being. He was also one of the most important figures in modern history. Hence I have included three overviews of the man and his contributions in order to give some perspective at the end. President Seymour's tribute is all the more weighty because he worked closely with Wilson at Paris. I will not comment on my own essay other than to say that I would not write it much differently were I composing it today instead of in 1962, when it was delivered as an address before the Presbyterian Historical Society in Philadelphia. Herbert Nicholas' article, by way of conclusion to this book, says some of the most sensible words ever pronounced about the relevance of the Wilsonian heritage for the problems of our own time.

I am grateful to Mrs. David Donald for inviting me to participate in this series, for permitting me to deviate somewhat from the format of the series, and, above all, for being a helpful editor. I am also indebted to my colleague in *The Papers of Woodrow Wilson,* Dr. William M. Leary, Jr., for help in gathering materials and copy editing this book. Some of the selections that follow had footnotes. I have deleted most of them and added a few of my own when I thought they were absolutely necessary.

ARTHUR S. LINK

Montreat, North Carolina
June 29, 1967

Woodrow Wilson, 1856-1924

Thomas Woodrow Wilson (he dropped his first name in early manhood) was born in Staunton, Virginia, on December 29, 1856, the son of the Reverend Dr. Joseph Ruggles Wilson and Janet Woodrow Wilson. Woodrow Wilson attended private schools and Davidson College, was graduated from the College of New Jersey (now Princeton University) in 1879, studied law at the University of Virginia in 1879–1880, and did graduate work in history, economics, and political science at The Johns Hopkins University from 1883 to 1885, receiving the Ph.D. from that institution in 1886.

Wilson taught at Bryn Mawr College (1885–1888), at Wesleyan University (1888–1890), and at Princeton (1890–1902). During this period he emerged as a leading political scientist, historian, and general writer, publishing (among other works) *Congressional Government* in 1885, *The State* in 1889, *Division and Reunion* in 1893, and *A History of the American People* in 1902. His last scholarly work, *Constitutional Government in the United States,* was published in 1908.

Elected president of Princeton University in 1902, Wilson led a general movement to upgrade that institution by reorganizing the curriculum, introducing new teaching methods, and enriching the faculty. Failure to achieve social reorganization of undergraduate life and a bitter dispute over the construction of a graduate college caused Wilson to resign in 1910.

In that same year Wilson was elected Governor of New Jersey. His success in winning reform legislation led to his nomination for the Presidency by the Democratic party and to his election to that office in 1912, in large part because the Republican party was split by the bolt of Theodore Roosevelt. From 1913 to 1915 Wilson and a Democratic Congress enacted what is called the New Freedom program. Aimed at expanding economic opportunity and encouraging competition, it included tariff reduction, establishment of the Federal Reserve System, and new antitrust legislation. In 1916, in part to win additional support, Wilson won adoption of legislation entailing more direct federal participation in economic and social affairs, including the first federal child-labor act, federal rural credits, and the eight-hour day for railroad workers. Re-elected by a narrow margin in November, 1916, Wilson sought to mediate the First World War, only to see his own country drawn into the conflict in April, 1917, on account of an all-out German submarine campaign against merchant shipping.

Wilson gave vigorous leadership in mobilizing the American people and the economy for a total war effort against Germany. He also quickly emerged as the chief spokesman of the hopes of liberals everywhere for a just and lasting peace settlement. The war ended in German defeat on November 11, 1918, and Wilson went to Paris to the Peace Conference to fight personally for his program. This program, embodied most succinctly in Wilson's Fourteen Points Address of January 8, 1918, included an end to secret alliances, a settlement of colonial claims with keen regard for the people involved, restitution of Belgium, return of Alsace-Lorraine to France, autonomy for the subject peoples of the Austro-Hungarian and Ottoman empires, nonintervention in the Russian civil war, and establishment of a League of Nations. He won only part of his objectives in the Treaty of Versailles, but deeply embedded in that treaty was Wilson's great hope for the postwar world—the League of Nations.

Having lost control of Congress in 1918, Wilson became embroiled in a controversy with Republicans over ratification of the Treaty of Versailles. He made a strenuous speaking tour of the West in September, 1919, only to suffer a severe stroke. The Senate refused to consent to ratification of the treaty, largely because Wilson and his chief Republican opponent, Senator Henry Cabot Lodge of Massachusetts, could not reconcile their differences. Wilson, an invalid in retirement, died at his Washington home on February 3, 1924, and was buried in the Washington Cathedral.

Wilson married Ellen Louise Axson of Georgia on June 24, 1885. They had three daughters—Margaret, Jessie, and Eleanor. Ellen Axson Wilson died on August 6, 1914. Wilson married Edith Bolling Galt of Washington on December 18, 1915.

A.S.L.

WOODROW WILSON

Growing Up in Georgia

In the spring of 1858, Thomas Woodrow Wilson being then two years old, the family moved to Augusta, Georgia, where the father was to be pastor of the Presbyterian Church for the next four years. . . .

The city of Augusta in the decade 1860–1870 was a community of about fifteen thousand souls. It was not as distinctively Southern a city as might be imagined, being then a place of rolling mills, furnaces, railroad shops, where the cotton trade also flourished, and cotton spinning mills were busy.

The First Presbyterian Church stood, as it stands today, in the middle of a lot occupying an entire square on Telfair Street. (Today, the Telfair Sunday-school building has been built by the side of the old church.) The church was, and is, a dignified and even imposing edifice. It was, and is, surrounded by a beautiful grove. The congregation was the most influential, in point of numbers and wealth, in the city. The sewing circle was a social factor among the ladies of Augusta. The Sunday school, which then met in a building at the corner of Ellis and McIntosh streets,

From William Bayard Hale, *Woodrow Wilson: The Story of His Life* (New York: Doubleday, Page & Company, 1912), pp. 23–40. Copyright 1912 by Doubleday, Page & Company; reprinted by permission of William Harlan Hale.

was a large one. Its superintendent became the Reverend Mr. Wilson's brother-in-law; he was Mr. James W. Bones.

Diagonally across from the church was the parsonage—a two-story, brick building, rather a mansion in proportions, surrounded by stable, outbuildings, and wall, all of red brick.

Tommy Wilson's earliest recollected impression had to do with the breaking out of the Civil War. On a certain day in November, 1860, the little boy, playing on the gate before his father's house, saw two men meet on the sidewalk and heard one of them cry: "Lincoln is elected, and there'll be war!" This is the earliest recollection of Woodrow Wilson. Something in the shrill tone of the speaker struck for the first time a chord of lasting memory.

Yet Woodrow Wilson remembers little, almost nothing, of the war. Augusta was on an island around which flowed the current of the conflict. It was never occupied by federal troops until Reconstruction days. No refugees ever fled to it. The man does remember that the boy saw a troop of men in every sort of garb, mounted on every sort of horse, ride past the house one day on their way to join the Confederate Army. They were not a terrifying or glorious spectacle. The boy cried after them in a slang exclamation of the day: "Go get your mule!"

He does remember the scarcity of the food supply that came on as the war progressed. Not that there was not enough food, but it was greatly restricted in variety. The restriction was not always unhappy, for it encouraged the ingenuity of housekeepers and taught them the edible quality of some things heretofore scorned. The delicious taste of the soup made from the cowpeas, previously fed only to the cattle, lingers to this day in the mouth of the little boy who tasted it.

Once when rumors came into the city of an approaching army (Sherman was threatening Augusta), a company of gentlemen armed themselves and marched valiantly out of town in the direction of the oncoming host. They lay all night on their arms in the woods and probably had a very enjoyable picnic of it, while their wives and families were waiting anxiously at home for news. The son of the Presbyterian pastor remembers the anxiety, the prayers, the unextinguished lamp in the parsonage all night. The brave defenders of their homes and firesides returned unensanguined; the army never came.

Wilson remembers a little pile of plug tobacco boxes of thick wood, tightly clamped with tin, reposing in a corner of the attic, growing in size from time to time. These were days when careful stewards were putting all their space resources into cash or the equivalent of cash for savings, and the funds of not a few were turned into plug tobacco, that being an asset easily convertible into money. The parson, too, had his little hoard of gold.

There was another war event that made its impression upon the boy: In the summer of '65 he saw Jefferson Davis ride by, under guard, on his way to Fortress Monroe.

After '65, Dr. Wilson's church was occupied temporarily by federal soldiers. However, such hardships as the city of Augusta suffered through the war were nothing compared with those endured in most parts of the South. It is to this fact that is to be attributed the small part in Woodrow Wilson's education played by the passions of the great conflict. He was only nine years old when the war ended. He was, too, apparently, a boy who somewhat tardily developed strong convictions. In short, he was a real boy while he was a boy, more concerned in the games of his crowd than in the principles of a war of which they saw little.

The Wilson boy was, his companions say, an active little fellow. It was a peculiarity that he was always running; he seemed incapable of proceeding from point to point otherwise. He can scarcely be said to have walked until he was fourteen or fifteen years old.

One of the thrilling moments of the boy's early life was the day and evening when the first streetcar came down the streets of Augusta. The cars were of the bobtail variety with a box for nickels up in front. At first, for the boys, the chief use and purpose of this new wonder was the manufacture of scissors out of crossed pins laid on the track. By night—the electric light had not then turned night into day—the glimmering red, purple, and green lights carried by the cars afforded endless pleasure as they approached and receded. The boys, too, made friends with the drivers and went along with them on their trips, being allowed sometimes to work the brakes and to turn the switches.

A little later Tom learned the delight of the saddle. Dr. Wilson kept a big black buggy horse, which Tommy used to ride—"conservatively," says his old playmate, Pleasant A. Stovall, now president and editor of the *Savannah Press* and one of the leading men of the state. Pleasant Stovall was prone to get many a tumble as the two lads rode through the streets and suburbs of Augusta, and used to wonder how his canny playmate got none.

The stable or barn and the lot enclosed by the parsonage offices were a favorite resort for all the boys of the neighborhood, among whom Wilson was a natural leader. He and Pleasant Stovall organized a club among the lads and called it the "Lightfoot Club." The chief activities of this fellowship seem to have been the playing of baseball with other nines of town boys and the holding of meetings characterized by much nicety of parliamentary procedure. Every one of the little chaps knew perfectly well just what the "previous question" was; knew that only two amendments to a resolution could be offered; that these were to be voted on in reverse order, and all the rest of it. The chief ornament of the clubroom was a highly colored presentation of his Satanic Majesty, originally an advertisement from a brand of deviled ham. The "Lightfoots" practiced and played occasional match games in the grounds of the Academy of Richmond County, on Telfair Street, just below the church.

The city of Augusta, founded by Oglethorpe, was a pleasant, even beautiful place, with its broad, well-shaded streets—one of them a boulevard on which stands a monument to Georgia's Signers of the Declaration—but rather wanting in bold or pic-

turesque features. The Savannah River at that point is broad, the
bank is barren, and the current heavy with red clay. As romantic a
spot as the city possessed was the grove in which the church
stood—a place of solemn shade and mysterious whisperings, often
the resort of the dreaming boy.

In the neighborhood of the town, at the point now called
Summerville, was a delightful suburban spot, then known merely
as the "Sand Hills," where Wilson's uncle, James Bones, who had
married Marion Woodrow, Woodrow Wilson's aunt, had a country
house. Wilson and Pleasant Stovall used to ride out to the Sand
Hills on horseback and spend a great deal of their time in the
pleasant country. Mrs. Wilson frequently spent a summer in the
North, and when she was away from home the boy went out to live
with his aunt in the Sand Hills.

The daughter of the house, Jessie Woodrow Bones (she is now
Mrs. A. T. H. Brower of Chicago), was a great tomboy and
idolized her cousin, and the two spent many a long happy summer
day at play in the woods. Long before she knew a letter, he had
filled her mind and imagination with the "Leather Stocking Tales,"
and what he read to her or told her in the twilight on the veranda
they acted out in their play next day. Casting aside all the
encumbrances of civilization except that which conservative authority in the shape of the aunt and mother required, they stained
their faces, arms, and legs with pokeberry juice and, with head-
dresses of feathers and armed with bows and arrows, crept out of
the house and stationed themselves by the side of a lonely road
leading from Augusta to a Negro settlement in the piney woods.
Here they would lie in wait until chance brought them their victims
in the shape of little darkies on their way to town with bundles of
lightwood on their heads. Then, with bloodcurdling war whoops,
they would dash out upon the unsuspecting prey, brandishing
wooden tomahawks in frightful fashion. The pair of youthful
savages never made any captives and had to console themselves by
remembering that kinky wool would not make attractive scalps to

hang at their belts. When no victims were forthcoming, little Jessie
had to impersonate the hated white man, and she was invariably
caught, made to run the gauntlet, scalped, and burned at the stake
by the bloodthirsty red man.

On other occasions, the little girl had to enact the part of
various kinds of game. Once she was supposed to be a squirrel in
the top of a tree. So good a marksman was her cousin that she was
hit by an arrow and came tumbling to the ground at his feet. The
terrified little hunter carried her limp body into the house with a
conscience torn as it probably never has been since, crying: "I am
a murderer. It wasn't an accident. I killed her." Young bones are
supple, and the little girl had happily sustained no injury.

Mr. Bones's house stood next to the United States Arsenal,
which, after the close of the war, was occupied by the federal
troops. Tommy and Jessie never tired of going to the guardhouse,
at the entrance to the arsenal grounds, to look at the soldiers and
talk with them. One day, however, Jessie's mother explained to her
that those friends of theirs were Yankees and had fought against
the South. It was a great blow to the couple, and they often
discussed the feasibility of converting the Yankees into Presbyterians—all good people being Presbyterians and all wicked ones
Yankees.

Tom Wilson, for one reason or another, was not taught his
letters until long past the date at which most youngsters have
learned to read. It may have been that his mother, who had been
strenuously taught in her young years in England and who used in
later life to speak feelingly of the folly of having to learn Latin in
one's sixth year, had ideas of her own about forcing the young
intellect. It may have been his father, who was a man of very great
positiveness and originality of opinion, was averse to having his
son get his first glimpses into the world of knowledge otherwise
than through himself. But, however it came about, Tom Wilson
was not taught his alphabet until he was nine years old. There was
a great deal of reading aloud in the family, not only his father and

mother, but his two sisters* frequently reading him choice extracts from standard books. Sir Walter Scott and Dickens were made familiar to the lad in this way: he remembers still the pleasure which his father showed in "Pickwick," reading the installments aloud, with Mrs. Wilson as the special audience, though even at the early age of eight the boy remembers that he appreciated much of the humor of the young author—just as Dickens himself asserted that at the same age he appreciated the humor of some of the situations which he later recorded in *Pickwick Papers.*

The lad attended the best schools Augusta offered. Public schools were either nonexistent or so poor as to be worthless, so the boy was put at an institution kept by Professor Joseph T. Derry, with a habitation over the post office on Jackson Street. Its pupils played in the old "burnt lot" near the bell tower. Later, Professor Derry moved his school to a building on the river bank next to some cotton warehouses. Here the boys made the warehouses their playgrounds, exploring and playing hide-and-seek among the cotton bales. It is still a recollection that the youngsters of that day, when bent upon some boyish prank, found that a pad gathered from the cotton bales was an effective protection from deserved punishment. . . .

But young Wilson's real instructor during the Augusta days was his father. Long before the age at which boys are imbibing knowledge from books he was already receiving from the lips of his father an education more varied, more practical and sound than any that could otherwise have come to him.

Father and son were constant companions, but it was Sunday afternoons that the elder devoted particularly to his son's training. Then, sitting on the floor, or rather reclining there against an inverted chair, the gifted parson poured out into the ears of the spellbound lad all the stores of his experience, learning, and thought. He was a man of wide information on the affairs of the world, a judge of good literature, a master of the queen of the

* Annie and Marion [ed.].

sciences, theology, and, withal, a man of much imaginative power —mingling with the warp of sound and well-founded thought the woof of picturesque fancy. Above all, the elder Wilson had a clean-working mind. He had a way of recognizing facts, and the processes of his thought dealt with them in the light of reason. If the boy had learned nothing else, he would have been happy indeed to have been guided from the beginning into the ways of clear, cold thinking.

And Dr. Wilson was a master of the English language. He believed that nobody had a thought until he could put it quickly and definitely into words. This he did himself, and this he taught his son to do. So that when the boy came to learn the written symbols in which speech is set down he was learning only a method of recording and transmitting a language which he already was well able to handle.

On Mondays the father would almost without exception take his son out with him on some excursion in the city or neighboring country. On a Monday the two would visit the machine shops; Tom would be shown furnaces, boilers, machinery; taught to follow the release of power from the coal to the completion of its work in a finished product of steel or of cotton. He remembers to this day the impression made upon him then by the gigantic engines, the roar of furnaces, or the darting up of sheets of flame; he remembers great forges presided over by sooty faced imps. In this fashion, by a continual round of visits of inspection in which the sight of visible things and visible processes was the text of running lectures on the principles of nature, chemistry, physics, and of the organization of human society, the boy learned what he would have had great difficulty in learning from books alone.

ARCHIBALD W. PATTERSON

✪

At the University of Virginia

My own acquaintance with this "man of destiny" began in the fall of 1879 (Session 1879–1880) when he entered the University of Virginia as a law student, having just completed his academic course at Princeton. He then signed himself "T. W. Wilson." The T stood for Thomas, and he was called "Tom" or "Tommy" by a few of his early associates. He called me "Patterson" or, more frequently, "Pat," and sometimes "Senator," a sobriquet given me by the South Carolina boys, out of compliment to a carpetbag Senator in that state who bore my name. While at "Virginia" he changed his signature to "T. Woodrow Wilson." Not until after leaving there did he drop the first initial, nor did I ever hear him say why this was done.

It is interesting to note that Grover Cleveland, the man whom Wilson most admired at one time, did the same thing, his name until late in life being Stephen Grover Cleveland. And this reminds me: In old Nassau Hall one day Wilson (then Princeton's president) took me into the Board Room and, pointing to a chair at the far end of a long table, said: "There is where Cleveland sits—

From Archibald W. Patterson, *Personal Recollections of Woodrow Wilson and some Reflections Upon His Life and Character* (Richmond: Privately Printed, 1929), pp. 6–19. Copyright 1929 by Archibald W. Patterson. Reprinted with permission of the author's daughter, Elizabeth Patterson Moyler.

9

the biggest man, taken all in all, it was ever my privilege to know."

At the time of Wilson's matriculation at "Virginia," he was about twenty-three years of age. Never physically robust, he was then rather thin, and his reddish complexion, together with a slight cutaneous affection, gave evidence of the dyspeptic trouble which followed him through life. Owing to this faulty digestion, he dieted himself very strictly, showing great self-control in the practice of such abstinence. Although fond of athletics, and never missing a good ball game when it was possible to see one, he took no part in the manly sports for lack of physical qualification.

It is said of Lord Coke that his ability to present a cause was first noticed when he was selected by his fellow students to make an argument to the benchers of the Inner Temple as to the poor quality of the food. Wilson's first speech at the university was made in the old gymnasium on East Range, shortly after his arrival, when presenting a medal to the successful athlete in an acrobatic performance. The leading contenders in that event were Gessner Harrison Smith, brilliant son of Professor Francis H. Smith; Eugene C. Massie, then of Charlottesville, later a prominent member of the Richmond bar; Sam Porcher, of South Carolina, and Tom Phister, of Maysville, Kentucky, who afterward became a judge in that city. The coming Kentucky jurist outstripped his rivals by common consent, and it was to him that the future President delivered a shining trophy. To nearly all those present Wilson was an entire stranger, and when he rose to speak the general inquiry went around, "Who is he?" His opening sentences captivated the audience, and he had spoken only a few minutes when his reputation as an orator was established. In the Jefferson Literary Society he took a lively interest from the outset, attending its sessions with noticeable regularity and often participating in the debates, not only on the stated topics but on issues arising out of the business proceedings which sometimes became spirited and impressive. "The Jeff," as we called it, was an excellent school of dialectics and parliamentary law. Wilson was especially happy in suggesting subjects for discussion. Instead of the hackneyed ones, so often debated on the academic hustings, he would insist upon having some fresh and practical theme about which people were thinking. This led to a reading of the daily papers and current periodicals by many who otherwise would not have known what was going on in the world. He immediately succeeded me as secretary of the "Jeff" Society. . . .

Wilson's class work was a matter of secondary importance. Though systematic in attendance upon lectures and never quite unprepared, lesson study and recitation seemed to be a sort of treadmill process, lacking the enthusiasm always exhibited in his forensic and literary endeavors. He paid little attention to examinations and did not apply for his degree. The law course at that time could be, and was frequently, made in one year. Wilson took the 1879–1880 course and returned in the fall of 1880, but on account of ill health left before the end of the second session.

He was in no sense a "mixer." Though known and admired by all as a man of mark, and having many acquaintances, formed by fraternity and other contacts, his circle of familiar friends was small. Those closest to him were Charles W. Kent, afterward Professor of English in the University; R. Heath Dabney; and, myself, the four of us customarily walking together for exercise whenever circumstances permitted. Sometimes Walter Lefevre or Walter D. Toy, later professor at Wake Forest, would join the party. On these strolls Wilson was at his best. Putting aside the reserve which characterized his general bearing, he would yield himself utterly to fun and frolic, like a boy out of school. He had an inexhaustible store of anecdotes and was a very prince of story tellers, always suiting the action to the word. When in one of these moods, he was as good as a circus. I often thought what an incomparable actor he would have made. Having a wonderfully mobile countenance, his facial expression at times was too ludicrous for description. On the other hand, when in a more serious vein, he could do the tragic part with equal effect. But he preferred comedy. He loved nothing better than a smart joke, but his jokes were never of the off-color variety. There was such cleanness and propriety in his fun-making that no one ever ventured to tell a risqué anecdote or use questionable language in his presence. He did not dance, smoke, drink or play cards, yet his attitude toward those who thought fit to indulge in such things had in it nothing of intolerance or censoriousness. Though squaring his practice with the ideals which he professed, no one could take him for a prude or a puritan. On the contrary, as we have seen, his temper was mirthful and he enjoyed a *bon mot,* even at his own expense. While Governor of New Jersey he spoke at the laying of a cornerstone for the Y.M.C.A. building in Atlantic City. It was his first public appearance after receiving the Democratic nomination for President of the United States. Former Postmaster General John Wanamaker introduced him as "a plain man and a learned statesman." The Governor began his speech by saying that the introduction, especially the "plain man" part of it, reminded him of his favorite limerick:

> For beauty, I am not a star,
> There are others more handsome by far;
> But my face, I don't mind it,
> For I am behind it;
> There are others in front that I jar.

After his election as President, he spoke in his native city of Staunton, where the people gave him a great ovation. Referring afterward to this occasion, he told the following story:

A small boy in the crowd shoved and pushed his way to the front until he stood squarely before the speaker, and shouted out "Where is it? Where is it?" The President stopped his speech and said good naturedly: "Well, my boy, I guess I'm it." "Pshaw!" responded the youngster, with a look of utter disgust, "I thought it was a dogfight!"

A joke which has since become somewhat familiar, I heard for the first time from him, with whom I am inclined to think it originated. It was about the fellow who went into a store to buy a clock. Pointing to one on the shelf, the dealer said: "That clock will run eight days without winding." "Fine," said the customer, "and how long will it go if you wind it?"

I asked him one day about the success of his History.* He laughed and said: "I have reason to believe it is growing in popularity and will prove a useful work. Walking along the street last week I saw a faker at the corner selling patent medicine. He was standing on a box marked 'Wilson's History of the American People.' If all the fakers in the country buy this book I ought to be satisfied, don't you think so?" By the way, the author was never particularly proud of this work. He confessedly wrote it, not so much to interest others as to instruct himself. There was no better way, he thought, to learn the fundamental facts and tendencies in the life of his own country than to study and interpret them in some systematic fashion. That is to say, this historical exercise was only a training for the great task which he had proposed as his chief objective. It was fine for him, he said, but hard on the public.

Even after he had been sorely smitten, when he was no longer his old self, the spirit of fun would now and again flare up with pathetic insistence. It is reported that at President Harding's funeral, while Wilson was sitting in his car waiting for the procession to move, a policeman, who did not recognize the sick man, stepped up to him and asked: "Can you tell me whether Senator Lodge has arrived?" Now, the Senator from Massachusetts was a most implacable enemy of the ex-President, and his severest critic. Wilson looked at the officer with a drawn smile and said, "I am not Mr. Lodge's keeper." Then he added this other timely limerick:

> I am not from the State of Massachusetts—
> The land of the *fish,* known as cod,
> Where the *Cabots* talk only to Lodges,
> And the Lodges talk only to God.

* *A History of the American People* (5 vols., 1902) [ed.].

Without adding other instances, what has been said will suffice to illustrate the keen sense of humor with which our friend was blessed. For it was indeed a blessing. He found his chief relaxation from intensive work in these sprees of jollity and good fellowship. Such a temperament would naturally enjoy the stage, and so it was that he frequently attended the theater, choosing to see a minstrel or vaudeville show rather than the heavier castes. In this way, as is well known, he sought an antidote for the cares of official life in Washington, and even as an invalid he occasionally appeared at Keith's.

Any account of the lighter and more human qualities of Wilson would be incomplete without some reference to his fondness for music. He had an excellent tenor voice and one of his first activities on reaching the university was to join the chapel choir and assist in organizing a glee club. These were two important institutions. The choir, composed of mixed voices, sang at the regular Sunday services. It was well trained, not only for rendering the hymns, but also for solo work and other special numbers. On Commencement Sunday the program was quite elaborate. But the glee club enjoyed still greater distinction. Membership in it was considered quite an honor, and the fortunate fellows received all sorts of attentions not accorded to the voiceless crowd. There were eight of us. In other words, it was an octette, made up as follows:

First tenors—Duncan Emmett, Woodrow Wilson.
Second tenors—Charles W. Kent, J. W. G. Blackstone.
First bass—A. B. Guigon, George P. DuBose.
Second bass—Syl. Stokes, A. W. Patterson.

Most of us knew little about the science of music, but Emmett, our leader, was a fine drillmaster, who soon had his recruits doing pretty good work. After a little while we began to give serenades under the windows of certain choice spirits, these nocturnal excursions taking us sometimes to Charlottesville and several miles out in the country. The season closed with a grand concert in the

Town Hall. This was really a brilliant affair. It came off on the night of the "Final Ball," and all the dancers, attending in full dress, made the occasion a memorable one.

That was in the days when Miss Randolph rightly boasted of having the choicest girls' school in America, at Edge Hill just below Charlottesville. Her catalogue scintillated with the names of famous belles and beauties, among whom were Minnie Anderson, afterward the celebrated Mrs. Willie Allen; Page Aylett, who became Mrs. William L. Royall; Genie Massie, first wife of Senator Oscar W. Underwood; Emily Buford, now Mrs. Clem Manly; the two lovely Carter sisters, Juliet and Anne, who respectively married Robert E. Lee, Jr., and Rosia Dulaney; and a host of others little less distinguished. "Edge Hill" was guarded against profane intrusion by many barriers, but "stony limits could not keep love out"; and so those angels of light came with their best beaus to transform that dingy old auditorium into a paradise of gladness and glory. Whatever may have been the quality of our music, the concert in other respects was a signal success. I am reminded just here of a joke gotten off that evening by the future President on Stokes and myself. One of the songs being pitched too low, the second basses had difficulty in touching bottom, which caused a smile among those who realized the situation. In the succeeding intermission, other members of the "troupe" were teasing the bassos, when Wilson said, "Yes, they made a mute reference to that low note."

One feature of Virginia University life at the time of which I am speaking has unfortunately passed away. I refer to the social intercourse between students and faculty in the homes of the several professors. . . . On Sunday evenings after chapel service it was customary for members of the choir and their friends to gather at Dr. Minor's* and sing until a late hour. In this connection I think particularly of Kent, Harding Walker and Wilson. The Minor family circle was a large one, consisting, among others, of several

* John B. Minor, distinguished Professor of Law [ed.].

young ladies, whose personal charm and sweet hospitality gave to
these meetings a character all their own, and never to be forgotten
by any participant. The venerable law teacher was generally with
us, his good gray head and cheery smile enhancing our pleasure by
the assurance of such high approval.

I have already alluded to Wilson's connection with the Jefferson
Society. Here was an arena in which his talents shone to special
advantage, and as he put most of himself into this society, so he
carried away from it the richest fruits of his industry. Probably the
personnel of "The Jeff," as already indicated, was never better
than at the time in question. The debates were of a uniformly high
order, and there was much speculation as to who would prove
their superiority in the end. The society awarded two medals, one
to the best debater and another to the best orator. In point of fact,
they were regarded simply as a first and second prize. The decision
rested with a committee of the faculty, who sat in judgment at the
final contest. This was an anomalous arrangement, instituted by
the university authorities because of the fraternity influence and
college politics, which had made an award of such honors by
popular vote little less than a farce. The faculty plan was a decided
improvement, though not altogether satisfactory. As the session
advanced, it became quite evident who would be the contestants in
the great debate. Set for April 2, 1880, the question at issue was:
"Is the Roman Catholic Element in the United States a Menace to
American Institutions?" And the alignment of speakers was as
follows:

Affirmative—Wm. Cabell Bruce and Benj. L. Abney.
Negative—Woodrow Wilson and J. M. Horner.

Mr. Bruce is now a United States Senator from Maryland;
Abney, lately deceased, became an eminent South Carolina attor-
ney and Horner rose to be a bishop of the Episcopal Church in
North Carolina. Bruce opened for the affirmative, Wilson for the
negative, and these were followed by Abney and Horner in their

order. The hall was packed almost to suffocation with an audience from far and near. Needless to describe the combat. When all was over the faculty committee, headed by Dr. John W. Mallet as chairman, submitted the following report:

The committee of the faculty selected by your society to judge of the debates for the prizes of the society, beg leave to report as follows:

While the general character of the debate in question has been very creditable to the speakers and to the society they represent, two of the contestants have shown remarkable excellence. Being required to decide between these gentlemen, our committee is of the opinion that the medal intended for the best debater should be awarded to Mr. Bruce.

In deciding that the position of orator to the society, with the other medal bestowed therewith, should be awarded to Mr. Wilson, our committee desires to express very high appreciation of his merits, not merely as a speaker, for which this honor is bestowed, but as a debater also.

The sequel is noteworthy. On the coming in of this report, Wilson showed disappointment and indicated his purpose to decline the orator's medal, saying that he made no pretensions to oratory; that he was a debater or nothing; and that his acceptance of such a trophy would be absurd. As above stated, the orator's medal was considered a second-best honor, and Wilson wanted the first or none. However, his friends, though feeling aggrieved by the award, urged him to acquiesce in it, which he finally did. . . .

The next college event in which Wilson participated came off in June, 1880, when the "Final Exercises" of our society were held, according to custom, in the spacious assembly hall or auditorium, which was then in a four-story wing or annex, adjoining the Rotunda on the north. This annex was destroyed by fire October 27, 1895, and never rebuilt, being succeeded by what is now known as Cabell Hall, some distance away. On this commencement occasion our two prize men spoke to an immense crowd and acquitted themselves handsomely. This was not a debate, of course, but set addresses made in acknowledgment of the honors conferred, each speaker choosing his own theme. I have forgotten, and Senator Bruce tells me that he does not recall, what were the subjects discussed by them respectively, nor is there any record to enlighten us upon this particular point. In the October (1880) University Magazine (Vol. XX, pp. 50–52) appears the following:

On Tuesday night (June twenty-ninth) came the long-looked for and long-talked about celebration of the Jefferson Society. President Thom presented the Debater's Medal to that highly-gifted and brilliant young man, W. Cabell Bruce of Virginia, who in his usual happy manner accepted the high honors conferred upon him by the Jefferson Society in a speech of well-chosen and graceful words.

Then to Mr. T. W. Wilson of North Carolina, President Thom delivered the Orator's Medal. The delivery of this medal to the Gladstone-like speaker of the University elicited one of the clearest, soundest, most logical, and thoroughly sensible addresses ever pronounced here at the University by a man so young. It was head and shoulders above the average efforts of college men, and won the applause of persons highly capable of passing an impartial judgment.

The scene is vividly impressed upon my mind even after all these years. The speakers presented a striking contrast to each other, as well in appearance as in their modes of thought and manner of delivery. Bruce was tall and sparely built, with the face of a poet, the head of a statesman, and rather fiery in his elocution. Wilson, much lower of stature, but erect and firm on his feet, and displaying an iron jaw and searching eyes, suggested a mighty force which found expression in masterful logic and faultless periods. In strength and simplicity his style could not be excelled. He loved the Anglo-Saxon tongue and would rarely use a word of other derivation unless driven to it by sheer necessity. When commended on one occasion for the singular virility of his utterances, he explained it by saying that he owed this achievement entirely to his father, who would always stop him in any carelessness or impropriety of speech and require a choice of words most apt for his purpose, advising the use of monosyllables as far as possible.

There was like rivalry between Bruce and Wilson for the

magazine writer's medal. In the volume above-mentioned, we find that the following evening, Wednesday, June 30, at the joint celebration of the Jefferson and Washington societies,

Prof. Francis H. Smith, Chairman of the Faculty Committee selected for the purpose of awarding, to the writer of the best article that had appeared in the pages of the Magazine, a gold medal, proceeded to deliver his decision. This was most ably and wittily done, and, of course, gave in the main general satisfaction. "John Randolph of Roanoke: a Sketch," was the article chosen, and W. Cabell Bruce, the honored writer, who in a short and well-timed speech received the glittering prize. Unstinted praise was given by the committee through its chairman, Professor Smith, to those excellent articles on John Bright and Mr. Gladstone, written by T. Woodrow Wilson of North Carolina. . . .

Following commencement festivities, which culminated in the "Final Ball," there was the usual exodus. Wilson had matriculated from Wilmington, North Carolina, and to the Old North State he now went for his vacation, promising to come back in the fall. Among the first to enroll for the class of 1880–81 was our "Jeff Orator" who took up his various lines of work with the same steadiness as before. He was already a publicist, and some of his best writing was done at this time, though he did not give it to the press until a much later date.

Wilson had a room on the ground floor in House F, Dawson's Row, which looked out upon the Reservoir road, a popular thoroughfare. I well remember how, in passing along this road, Wilson might be seen busily engaged in preparing some literary production, and when in mild weather the windows were open, he would stop long enough to jolly those on the outside, or lay down his work and join his friends in a "constitutional." I recall too that he always wrote with a gold pen (not of the fountain variety, which came into vogue later), and that his manuscripts were models of neatness and penmanship. When taking notes in class he wrote shorthand and did so with no little facility. There is an impression on my mind that the stenographic method so employed was one of his own contrivance. As soon as typewriting became an established fact, Wilson bought a machine and became very proficient in its use. After this, the pen and ink were largely discarded except for signing his name.

As already stated, Wilson did not stay through his second year. On account of sickness he retired from the Law School and went home in midsession. We corresponded after his departure and upon my invitation he returned for "Final Week," during which time he stayed with me. My room was on West Range, the one occupied by Edgar Allan Poe in his day, and next door was that of "Willie" Bruce, who had a habit of rehearsing his speeches therein without regard to the peace and dignity of the neighborhood.

Upon leaving the university, Wilson "swung out his shingle" as a lawyer in Atlanta, Georgia, but after trying it awhile, and realizing that the practice of law was not for him, he abandoned this field of endeavor and repaired to Johns Hopkins University where (1883–1885) he pursued a course of postgraduate work along historical lines.

✪

Young Teacher

Three decades before Fiume loomed large as an Italian problem, President Wilson once faced a different kind of an Italian problem, involving a monkey, a hand-organ player and the dignity of his classroom at Wesleyan University, in Middletown, Connecticut.

One of the members of his history class, Waters B. Day, now the dignified president of a New Jersey trust company, was then manager of the *Wesleyan Argus,* the college weekly newspaper; and his duties in getting out the paper on Wednesday afternoons always made him a half hour late at the history class, for which he had secured the proper standing excuse. One Wednesday on his way up the college hill to Professor Wilson's classroom, late as usual, he passed an Italian organ-grinder leading a monkey on a string and the brilliant idea occurred to him that Professor Wilson's class ought to be serenaded. The Italian's eyes fairly bulged when Day handed him a shining twenty-five cent piece and told him to wait for five minutes and then play a tune under yonder window and make the monkey climb up to the room on the vines outside.

Full of glee over the fun in store for everybody, Day marched

From Carl F. Price, "When Woodrow Wilson Was at Wesleyan," New York *Christian Advocate,* XCIV (August 7, 14, 1919), pp. 998–1000, 1030–1031. Copyright 1919 by *The Christian Advocate;* reprinted by permission.

into the classroom rather jauntily. But before he had taken his seat
the whole class was in an uproar of laughter. He turned around to
see what had happened and there—just inside the door, near the
professor's desk—stood Italian, monkey and organ, on which the
tousled artist began to grind forth one of the popular ditties of the
day. The poor, old Italian had not understood a word of Day's
instructions, except that he was to play a tune for the benefit of the
classroom. Of course, the class howled at this. But Professor
Wilson tried his best to look stern, and in stentorian tones exclaimed: "Day, take that fellow out of here at once!" The senior
obeyed meekly and took him by the arm to push him out. But the
Italian's feelings were wounded, and he turned on Day: "You give
me quarter and tell me play. I play!" And once more he whirled
the handle of the organ for a few more wheezing measures. Finally
Day managed with a show of indignation to get the fellow out and
to close the door, and he scampered back to his seat about as
confusedly as possible. All through the recitation he was on pins
and needles for, to make matters worse, he had not prepared his
recitation that day, and throughout the rest of the hour he was
afraid that the professor would call on him to recite and make a
monkey out of *him*. But Wilson was generous and saved the culprit
further embarrassment just then. At the close of the class hour,
Day realized that he must do something to set matters right with
Professor Wilson. So he conjured forth from his brain some
imagined perplexity about a point in the history lesson. After the
class had left the room he went up to the professor's desk and
asked him some diverting question. Wilson looked at him quizzi-
cally for a moment, and with a twinkle in his eyes said to him:

"Day, why this sudden interest in the subject of history? I
strongly suspect if that Italian had not marched in here with his
organ and monkey, you wouldn't have asked that question. But, if
this prank has served to increase your interest in the work of my
classroom and the subject of history in general, I shall be greatly
delighted, and we'll call our account square."

Many a professor would have insisted on a man's being disciplined for such a prank, but Wilson treated his students like men, and gained all the more respect from them on that account. One of his Wesleyan students once put it this way: "Every man in his class felt inspired to do his very best, not because of any exhortation or threat, or even suggestion, from Wilson himself, but from the very atmosphere of his personality; not a feeling of fear of consequences was present, but a feeling that you were ashamed if you were not at your best."

The two college years at Middletown, Connecticut, when he was Professor of History and Political Economy at Wesleyan University, marked a period in his life of great literary activity and mental development. But the restraints of later dignities had not yet been laid upon him, and in some of his enthusiasms he was still thoroughly youthful. At one of the varsity football games on the Wesleyan campus last fall a prominent graduate of twenty-six years ago was recalling memories of his old professor and expressed himself in this way: "My most vivid recollection of Woodrow Wilson was a tall, thin man running up and down these very sidelines during the afternoon's football practice, waving his closed umbrella in the air and cheering encouragement at the top of his lungs to the team on almost every play!"

In the classroom, however, there was nothing boyish about this enthusiastic new member of the faculty. Professor Wilson was a man among men. He never treated his students like schoolboys. Without losing his sense of humor, he had a happy fashion of dealing with them always as men, and insisting that they must always act as such.

Withal he was not averse to introducing a sparkling humor into his lectures or into the recitation hours. He rarely told a funny story, but spontaneous, witty remarks were not the exception. Perhaps this explains why the college annual, *Olla Podrida, '91,* contained in its department "As in a Looking-Glass" this thinly veiled allusion to him:

Prof. W-i-n.
A merrier man
Within the limit of becoming mirth
I never spent an hour's talk withal.

Once when the class was discussing the "persistence of the ego" and one junior was on his feet, reciting, Wilson naïvely asked him:

"Now, Mr. Abbott, are you not the same man you were last year—only with a few modern improvements?"

The whole class, professor, too, enjoyed a roar of laughter at this sally.

Once the laugh was at Wilson's expense and it came at the very first recitation of one of his classes, when he was making up the roll of the class. There was a man in the class by the name of Noe (pronounced as two syllables); and when the professor came to his name, he pronounced it with only one syllable. The possessor of the name arose and courteously corrected him, giving it with two syllables, No'e. With some embarrassment because of the mistake, Professor Wilson proceeded with the roll until he came to the name Roe. Not wishing to be caught this time, he pronounced it Ro'e, with two syllables. The laughter was so violent this time that it was a half minute before Roe could explain to the blushing professor that he belonged to the one-syllable category.

One morning, not many months after the birth of their daughter Eleanor (now Mrs. McAdoo), Professor Wilson entered the history class with a sleepy look on his face and prefaced his lecture with this remark:

"Gentlemen, if I do not lecture with my wonted brilliancy today, it will be because since three o'clock this morning I have been walking the floor with my baby."

Speaking one day in history class of one of the mad kings of England, he put the case in these words: "When he came to years of discretion, he was found to *have* no discretion." Another epigram of his, remembered from his classroom at Wesleyan, was this: " 'Business is business,' which is just another way of saying that business is not Christianity."

One of his first courses at Wesleyan before a group of students, until then strangers to him, he began in this fashion:

"I suppose you are all thinking: first, 'What manner of man is this?' and second, 'What good is he going to do me?' "

And these two points of view, whether subconsciously or otherwise, he kept before him in his work. He sought to impress the vigor and earnestness of his personality upon the boys, thus the better to make it possible to do them the good which he felt it was his business to do.

There were notably few cuts or absences from Professor Wilson's lectures, and rarely any "unprepared" slips, such as the students placed on a professor's desk on entering the classroom when they were not prepared to recite. Especially was the latter true after one occasion when most of the class handed in "unprepareds" on entering the room, and the professor, viewing this pile of papers on his desk, gave the boys this greeting: "Gentlemen, I had hoped you might emulate your Anglo-Saxon forefathers, who thought it not creditable to be 'unprepared' for anything!" As each lecture of his began, there was an air of expectancy throughout the class. And sometimes it happened that his students actually became so intensely interested in what he was saying that they forgot to take notes. "I can see him now," said one of the boys of those days, "with his hands forward, the tips of his fingers just touching the table, his face earnest and animated, many times illuminating an otherwise dry and tedious subject by his beautiful language and his apt way of putting things." . . .

His keen interest in the athletics of the college was one of the greatest factors in warming the heart of the undergraduate toward Professor Wilson. While a student at Princeton he had taken a prominent part in athletic affairs, and was referee and one of the directors of the Princeton football team in the days when the football championship resided on the campus of the Orange and

Black. It is said that at one time he was kept from playing on the victorious team only by a prolonged sickness.* Fortunately on Professor Wilson's arrival in Middletown his keen interest in football was deemed a valuable asset for the local team, and before the year was over he was made one of two members of the Advisory Board of the Wesleyan Football Association, the other member being Seward B. Coffin, '89, son of Senator O. V. Coffin, afterward Governor of Connecticut. All through the weeks of fall practice Professor Wilson served as one of the coaches for the eleven, ably assisting Captain H. D. Slayback, of New York City, in devising new plays of gridiron strategy.

As a result, in 1889, the University of Pennsylvania was defeated 10–2, Amherst 39–0, Williams College 20–17, Rutgers 58–4 and Trinity 6–0, these victories being interspersed here and there with some defeats (Princeton among them), which, of course, nobody at Wesleyan now cares to remember after the lapse of a quarter of a century. The victories, however, gave Wesleyan the primacy among the minor colleges of New England; and as Lehigh had gained a similar ascendancy among the smaller colleges of her section, great importance was attached in the football world to the Wesleyan-Lehigh game to be played at Hampden Park, in Springfield, Massachusetts, on Thanksgiving Day, 1889. In fact, the Lehigh supporters boasted that in case the laurels of victory came their way, they would insist upon demanding Wesleyan's coveted place in the old Intercollegiate Football Association, which included Harvard, Pennsylvania, Princeton, Yale and Wesleyan.

The great Puritan holiday brought a hard storm, and the day's battle was fought in a sea of mud. To the consternation of the Wesleyan "rooters," the Lehigh team developed an altogether unexpected strength, and the game was going their way. Twice Lehigh scored easy touchdowns, and it seemed as though Wesleyan faced certain defeat, when suddenly from the Wesleyan

* This might well have been "said." It was inaccurate [ed.].

bleachers a man walked out in front, clad in heavy rubber boots and a raincoat. He shouted to the Wesleyan contingent reproaching them for not cheering for their team; and at once began to lead them in the Wesleyan yell, beating time for them with his umbrella. This he continued violently until the Wesleyan cheers heartened Slayback's men, in spite of their handicap, and the tide of the game turned. The cardinal and black players felt the thrill of the Wesleyan spirit among their loyal supporters on the sidelines and before the game ended they had made two touchdowns themselves and tied the score. After the game the Lehigh men, inquiring about the magnetic cheer-leader, were informed that he was Wesleyan's Professor of History, Dr. Woodrow Wilson.

Professor Wilson's loyalty to his own alma mater and his enthusiasm as coach for the Wesleyan eleven were put to a severe test on Election Day, 1888, the date when Benjamin Harrison was elected to the office that the professor was destined later to fill; for on that date Princeton and Wesleyan matched strength and strategy on the gridiron, Walter Camp being referee of the game. But probably no college other than Princeton would Professor Wilson have accepted with equanimity that year to administer a defeat to Wesleyan.

II

The outstanding contribution that Professor Wilson made to the life of the college body as a whole was the founding of the House of Commons for purposes of debate and parliamentary practice. Up to that time a Wesleyan debating society had conducted its work in a desultory way; but Professor Wilson's innovation for a time at least put new life into the practice of debate. On January 5, 1889, he called the college body together and organized them into a House of Commons along the lines of the British Parliament. In explaining the new plan he called attention to the almost inevitable defects of the old college debating or literary society, which he

styled "a galvanic movement, stimulating life, but not life itself."
He added: "To argue on any side without the basis of conviction
of any sort is mental suicide"; and this sentence recalls the story
that when Wilson was a Princeton undergraduate and entered the
preliminary extemporaneous debate contest for the Lynde Debate
in Whig Hall he drew from the hat a piece of paper instructing him
to debate for Protection as against Free Trade. He immediately
tore the paper into bits and declared he would not stultify himself
by debating for a proposition that was against his convictions.
Thus he forfeited his right to contest for the prize.

In explaining the proposed House of Commons he continued:
"The function of our new organization is the function of debate.
To imitate the House of Representatives would be patriotic, but
not interesting. The House of Representatives does not do much of
its own debating, but refers most of its business to standing
committees; and if a committee recommends a measure the House
is likely to adopt it as a matter of course. So we shall imitate the
British House of Commons, thereby introducing a dramatic element, in that a body of ministers resigns when defeated. The
ministers will support the questions they believe in, and the natural
party line will arise without any arbitrary divisions. . . . It is this
which we seek, and we do not copy the House of Commons
because it is English, you know."

Great applause! Plan unanimously adopted by the college body.
No adverse remarks. And the following Tuesday was set for the
election of a Speaker. At that meeting the chairman *pro tem* was
Professor Wilson and the clerk Frederick M. Davenport, '89, now
New York State Senator. A constitution was adopted and Arthur
W. Partch, '89, was elected Speaker, who appointed as the first
ministry: Samuel G. Landon, '89; John Evan Jenkins, '91; and
Theodore S. Henderson, '92.

The new society began its work with great enthusiasm. Large
numbers of the college boys attended, and it was felt that its
democratic methods might counteract any partisan or fraternity

cliques that might exist in the college. After bylaws had been considered, the very first motion presented, namely, to limit each speaker to one speech and to ten minutes, was lost. And this was because Professor Wilson (called upon to give his opinion, though not a voting member of the body) stated that he favored giving each speaker unlimited time. "The House," said he, "is a body which can defend itself against anyone trying to impose on it. It has lungs, and the door is open. Slow men often have very good things to say and they are often worth waiting for." . . .

During his first year in Middletown the professor completed his book, *The State; a Sketch of Institutional History and Administration,* that was published by Heath & Co. It was most favorably received by the intellectual people of the town and in the college. The college *Argus* made this comment upon it: "One might suppose from a survey of the ground to be covered by such a work that its author would have a constant struggle with 'the fiend Dryasdust.' If there has been such a conflict, Professor Wilson has come off victor." Not long after its publication, Senator Hawley made an address in Middletown, Professor Wilson being in the audience. In the course of his address the Senator made a vigorous attack upon the new book, which was highly resented by Wilson's friends in the audience. The professor could not be prevailed upon that evening to make any comment but the next morning his class was privileged to hear his vigorous reply, that bore much logic, but little bitterness in it.

The Wilsons lived in a white frame house, originally built in the thirties by Professor Harvey B. Lane on High Street, where now stands the Eclectic Fraternity House. This was the street which Charles Dickens, on his visit to Middletown, styled "the most beautiful avenue in America." The Wilson home was convenient to the college buildings, being situated opposite the campus; but the house was regarded as far from convenient in its interior arrangements, being an old-fashioned building. When not in the classroom Wilson could usually be found sitting at his desk near the front

window working on his *History of the American People*.* While
this was a stupendous and engrossing task, he was never too busy
to attend to any of his college duties, or to listen to any of his
pupils who sought advice.

It was in this house that his daughter Eleanor was born and in
the afternoons the little lady and her mother were often to be seen
on the sloping lawn or the spacious back porch, that commanded a
glimpse of the Connecticut River. Judge D. Ward Northrup, then
postmaster in Middletown, was a near neighbor, living on Church
Street, the back portion of their yards being adjacent and the
Northrup boys and the Wilson girls, together with a nephew of the
professor, were frequent playmates.

Both the judge and Professor Wilson belonged to the Monday
Club† a select coterie of a score of Middletonians of culture, that
met on Monday evenings in some member's home. One of the
group at each meeting presented an elaborate paper upon some
theme announced in advance, and after the reading of the essay a
general discussion followed, in which every member took an active
part. Professor Wilson's share in these evenings of high converse is
still remembered by the few survivors of that intellectual group.

Within two years of his coming to Wesleyan University, Professor Wilson received a call to the Chair of Jurisprudence and
Political Economy at Princeton University and soon afterward
resigned from the Wesleyan faculty. His resignation was received
with profound regret. But it was not to be wholly unexpected; for
it is exceedingly difficult for a small college to hold all of its strong
teachers in the face of the attractions of larger colleges and larger
spheres of influence. Wesleyan has been fortunate in holding men
of great strength upon her faculty, who have loyally resisted the
allurement of the larger college, preferring to devote their lives to
Wesleyan, even at the sacrifice of larger salaries. Woodrow Wilson
was wholesomely ambitious for a larger career. One day he was

* Wilson must have been working on something else [ed.].
† Actually, the Conversational Club [ed.].

asked by a member of the Wesleyan faculty why he had dropped his first name. His reply was significant and prophetic:

"Because I believe that the name Woodrow Wilson will carry a man farther in a public career than the name Thomas Woodrow Wilson." His return to his alma mater, Princeton, as a full professor was a large step forward in the career he was seeking to achieve. And, although his departure from Wesleyan was regretted, it was attended by many expressions of respect and esteem.

Princeton Professor

The bitter controversies that were to center upon the personality of
Woodrow Wilson did not begin until after the nineties, when I was
no longer connected with the university and was under no necessity for taking sides. My most intimate friends in Princeton divided
into hostile camps, and their differences are no part of my story.
But since Wilson was destined to become a national figure and
then a world figure, I should like to set down my own impression
of his mind and character in the period when I saw much of him,
and when, fortunately, myth and legend and calumny had not
begun to distort the judgment of an observer.

When I first knew him, he was only thirty-six, but there was little
that was youthful in him except high spirits, energy, and self-
confidence. He had never, I suspect, been a boy of normal boyish
irresponsibility. His father, who often paid long visits to Princeton
and was a whimsical, forceful person, had been "Tommy's" real
comrade and had molded his mind and behavior. The son was a
true child of a manse where religion, wit, and political theorizing
went hand in hand. Both father and son were idealists, phrase-
lovers, and critics.

Wilson's family life was singularly happy. He was adored by his

From Bliss Perry, *And Gladly Teach* (Boston: Houghton Mifflin Company, 1935), pp. 153–159. Copyright 1935 by Houghton Mifflin Company;
reprinted by permission.

wife and daughters and by the Axson* and Howe† relatives who at
times filled the house. He was strict with his children, particularly
in regard to their habits of speech. While he had an extraordinary
fund of amusing dialect stories—Scotch, Negro, and Irish—his
children were enjoined rigidly from the use of slang. Sometimes
they echoed his own meticulous vocabulary without really understanding it. George Armour, a book-collecting neighbor of the
Wilsons, used to repeat with delight a conversation between the
small Wilson girls and his own daughter. "What is a dilettante?"
asked the Wilson child. "I don't know," confessed the Armour
child, "do you?" "No, but that is what my father says your father
is."

He was physically of an ascetic habit, and gave the appearance
of being trained rather fine. He provided wine and cigars for his
guests, but in the nineties his physician was forbidding him both
alcohol and tobacco. He took little exercise except bicycling, and
held himself to a stern schedule of solitary work in his study, which
was guarded sedulously by his idolizing wife. Yet in those years, if
not always later, he was extremely fond of company. He loved the
society of cultivated women, and treated them with an elaborate
Southern courtesy which was already beginning, toward the end of
the century, to seem a trifle old-fashioned in the North. But in him
it was genuine. For some years Mr. and Mrs. Wilson, Mr. and
Mrs. Hibben,‡ Mrs. Perry and I used to take tea with Miss Ricketts
on Sunday afternoons, and unless those talks are now idealized by
distance, they were exceptionally good. We rarely discussed politics. Wilson was, by the way, a great admirer of Cleveland,
though he had been perturbed by the truculent tone of the Vene-
zuela message. His review of Cleveland's second administration,
printed in the *Atlantic,* was one of the ablest contemporary

* The family of his wife Ellen Louise Axson Wilson [ed.].
† The family of his sister Annie Wilson Howe, of Columbia, South Carolina [ed.].
‡ Professor and Mrs. John Grier Hibben, among the closest friends of
the Wilsons in Princeton at this time [ed.].

tributes to Cleveland's public services. I think the two men would have remained warm friends at Princeton if they had not been estranged by meddlers and by sharply diverging views of what was best for the university; but all that belongs to a later period. What we debated over the tea cups was books and general theories of life. Our hostess was more widely read in European literatures than any of her guests, but Wilson usually outshone that little, intimate company in sheer inventiveness and pungency of phrase. I felt occasionally, not that he "talked for victory," but that he concentrated too much upon his own conversational game, much as some professional golfers content themselves with shooting steadily at par without regard to the shots of their opponents. This is perhaps a better rule for a golf match than for a tea party, though it was often more delightful to listen to Wilson than to challenge the soundness of his opinions. Miss Ricketts—to say nothing of her brilliant mother—was quite capable of doing that!

We usually walked down to the college chapel service after tea was over. Wilson took his turn in conducting it, and I think no one who listened to his chapel talks could have doubted the sincerity of his religious faith. The Wilsons, on coming to Princeton, had joined the unfashionable Second Presbyterian Church, thinking that they were more needed there than in the *"First"* Church which had been recommended to us by Professor Raymond. It was left to a later decade to invent the hypothesis that Wilson was a hypocrite in everything, including religion.

No one among his intimates—though the number of his real intimates was few—had any uncertainty, in the 1890's, as to Wilson's nobility of character. Of course he had his faults. Sometimes I found it hard to excuse his impatient contempt for the dullness and slowness of some of his elderly colleagues—particularly the "Three Snoozers" about whom West wrote a witty and privately circulated poem. His Scotch-Irish temper was quick and not always under perfect control. But his "arrogance" and "autocracy," like his "timidity" and "vacillation," were the invention of a later epoch. I sat on committees with him very frequently, and though he knew his own mind and never hesitated to express it, he betrayed no arrogance of opinion. In his extempore public addresses, and probably in his larger classrooms, his gift of eloquence sometimes led him into overstatements which in his quieter moods he would have been the first to criticize. I always thought, when I was his colleague, that he romanticized "affairs," that is to say, the practical business of the world. The word seemed to hypnotize him, as it had hypnotized two of his favorite authors, Burke and Bagehot. But I took this as a proof that he was a born college professor and was therefore inclined to exaggerate the significance of "affairs" which lay outside his range. I used to think also that he was rather too militaristic, inclined to romanticize the army and navy, and expending too much eloquence in praising American achievements because they were "American." But all this was mere difference of opinion between two friends.

No one, I venture to say, then thought him cold or selfish. It is true that he was absorbed, day by day, in his teaching and writing, and he had the gift of intense concentration upon the business in hand. He was already composing directly upon the typewriter, and defended warmly that method of composition. We discussed it more than once, for I was skeptical. I remember his saying: "When you find yourself at a loss for the right word, don't you light your pipe and walk across the room and perhaps look out of the window? You lose your concentration. Now I force myself to sit with my fingers on the keys and *make* the right word come." And he was sure that the word that came was right.

It is possible, of course, that the adulation of his classes and the general recognition among his associates of his superior gifts as a speaker and writer may have spoiled him a little; but I was never conscious of it. If he had at that time any hankering after executive leadership, either in the educational world or in politics, none of us knew it. His ideals for "the new Princeton" had been expressed in his oration at the "Sesqui," and when, in 1902, he was suddenly chosen to succeed President Patton, his colleagues almost without exception recognized the fitness of the choice. Yet so completely had he stood apart from all candidacy for actual office, that his election came as a surprise. I confess that I had thought of him as a man endowed by nature and training to originate theories of action and to express them with convincing skill, rather than to put them into actual operation.

The fault of the hero of tragedy, as Aristotle pointed out long ago, may be the excess of a virtue as well as the presence of a vice. If Wilson ever had any real vices, they were at least unknown to observers of his character during the "golden nineties." In my own opinion, his "tragic fault" lay in the excess of that self-confidence which was one of the most fascinating of his virtues. I have heard him quote with delight the saying that while a Yankee always thinks he is right, a Scotch-Irishman *knows* that he is right. And at forty, Woodrow Wilson had already had the long habit of success. As a student of government, as teacher, essayist, and orator, he had won brilliant and unquestioned rank. He had worked tirelessly in solitude, had held himself inflexibly to his task. He had learned self-reliance. He trusted his own logic and his own instincts without much counsel from other men. It is the ancient story of heroes—and of martyrs.

For the line between superb confidence and tragic overconfidence is often hidden from the hero himself. Wilson did not cross it until he became president of his university. On the larger issues of his policy in that office, I believe him to have been right, but the sense of his own rightness and conversely of the wrongness of his opponents began to rob him temporarily of his old skill in diplomacy, his tact and judgment and patience. He was so sure that the right must prevail that he forgot the stupidity and slowness of the average man, and underestimated the power of his opponents. I venture to quote a significant remark which he made to me shortly after his election to the presidency of Princeton. He was to address a gathering of teachers in Boston, and as I was working there, I

gave him a luncheon at the University Club, inviting President
Eliot, Charles Francis Adams, Richard Olney, Charles Eliot
Norton, Thomas Bailey Aldrich, Dr. Crothers, Judge Robert
Grant, and other men who were likely to interest him. Wilson was
never in better form or gayer spirits. He fascinated the Bostonians,
particularly the most fastidious of them all, Charles Eliot Norton.
After the luncheon I escorted him to the Trinity Place Station, to
put him on the train for New York. As we were waiting for it, he
spoke of his new work at Princeton, and said: "If West* begins to
intrigue against me as he did against Patton, *we must see who is
master!*" There was a grim smile with these words, as if he
doubted as little as I did who was master. But both of us were
wrong: in the subtleties of academic intrigue he was no match for
West, and the game went to the more resourceful player. It was
tragic overconfidence that brought disaster to Wilson's dreams for
Princeton, although that disaster, indirectly, made him Governor
of New Jersey and President of the United States.

* Andrew Fleming West, Dean of the Graduate School at Princeton and
Wilson's great and successful antagonist in a fierce battle over the location
of a graduate college [ed.].

✪

President of Princeton

In February, 1906, at the invitation of Wilson, I made the trip to Princeton from Baltimore, where I was teaching at what is now the Gilman School, for an interview. This led to my later call to the faculty at Princeton as a preceptor, in the spring of 1906. When I arrived at Prospect, Mrs. Wilson met me and told me that "Dr. Wilson had been ill with grippe, but was now much better and would see me in his bedroom." As always, he was charming and friendly. Wilson was still in bed, and when I came into the room he was reading a small book on some English literary figure by J. Churton Collins, which attracted my special attention as I had heard Collins lecture at Oxford some years before. According to my diary (February 16, 1906) there followed—"a most delightful talk for twenty minutes. A most attractive man."

Soon after my coming to Princeton in September, 1906, I was fairly closely associated with him at times as an assistant in his courses in jurisprudence and constitutional government. Also as a member of the Department of History, Politics and Economics, he often attended departmental meetings, and took a very active part in the discussions. Although Harry A. Garfield was then chairman

From William Starr Myers, "Wilson in My Diary," William Starr Myers (ed.), *Woodrow Wilson: Some Princeton Memories* (Princeton: Princeton University Press, 1946), pp. 37–51. Copyright 1946 by the Princeton University Press. Reprinted by permission of Princeton University Press.

of the department, Wilson, as everywhere at Princeton, was the dominating influence.

As an assistant in his courses to the undergraduates, I often sat in the back of the room to hear his lectures. He always was stimulating in his presentation. It may be frankly stated here that, after experience with some very great teachers, I consider Wilson the greatest classroom lecturer I ever have heard, just as Edwin A. Alderman, my teacher at the University of North Carolina (and later president of the University of Virginia), was the greatest master in class quizzing and discussion, and Herbert Baxter Adams, Wilson's own master, the greatest all-around teacher. This is my mature conviction after experience in my school, college, and university life. Wilson held his students spellbound, and at the close of a lecture they would often cheer him, not for the purpose of bootlicking, but because they just could not help it. His inspiration for students may be further explained by another diary note:

"WEDNESDAY, MAY 20, 1908.—This evening departmental meeting at Nassau Club. 'Woodrow' there, and had discussion of the preceptorial system. He made, as usual, pregnant remarks, such as—'our students too dependent in thought, look upon teachers as *authorities* rather than guides. A lecturer should make telling comparisons and stimulate hearers to thought, rather than describe things or attempt to teach them.' "

This same idea was earlier developed in Wilson's essay on "An Old Master" (Adam Smith), in his small volume of essays bearing the same name, and published in 1893.

Wilson was so persuasive that he often could make his hearers believe that black was white, and vice versa—at least while he was speaking. In fact, at the time of the controversy about the clubs in Princeton, the students told me they would not go to hear Wilson, because they knew they were right in their support of the clubs as then existing, and that "Woodrow would make them do the opposite thing, if they went to hear him, and that would be wrong." I told Wilson this, which much amused him, and he

mentioned it in subsequent addresses. Furthermore, it always has
been my opinion that his greatest speeches were made before he
went into practical politics. When a candidate for office, or an
officeholder, the danger of committing himself always was great.
As an educator, he could speak with greater freedom, and he
did.

One of the greatest of good fortunes had come to Wilson when
he married Ellen Louise Axson in 1885. Mrs. Wilson was a
woman of rare charm of person and manner, of fine perceptions,
of real ability, whose advice and devoted interest in his fortunes
was one of the dominating influences in his life. In fact, there are
many people who believe that a large part of Woodrow Wilson's
later success was made possible by the counsel, advice, and guidance of this devoted woman. Wilson was fairly worshiped by his
family, and she was the one who did not hesitate to tell him the
truth, as well as serve as a sort of balance wheel. It is a probability
that Mrs. Wilson's death in the White House at Washington in
August, 1914, removed this influence at the time when he most
needed it, and he then began that series of political mistakes which
were to cost him dear and lead to his final defeat and the political
disaster of his party. As always with a man in public life, envious
and hostile tongues slandered him, but those who knew him best
never gave credence to the stories concerning his private character,
which were without foundation.

Wilson's political views were often misunderstood. He was
brought up in the school of political thought common to the South
which was suffering at the time under the tragedy of "Reconstruction," rather than "Restoration," as Lincoln has intended. But it is
noteworthy that he wrote to Professor A. B. Hart under date of
June 8, 1889, as quoted by Ray Stannard Baker in the *New York
Herald Tribune* of October 17, 1927: "Ever since I have had
independent judgments of my own I have been a Federalist." The
following diary note may be of special interest here.

"FRIDAY, MAY 8, 1908.—This evening Politics Club entertained

by Paul van Dyke at his home. Subject, an open discussion on the
'Policies of Theodore Roosevelt.' President Wilson was present
and opened discussion by attacking Roosevelt, said his policies
meant substitution of government by commission, and executive
discretion for government by law. 'Woodrow' stated that he was
not a Jeffersonian Democrat, because no one knew what kind of a
Democrat Jefferson really was—that he [Wilson] agreed with him
in this particular, that government is a field for distrust, and he
distrusted Roosevelt's policies. A splendid discussion followed.
Garfield gave his opinions last (strongly pro-Roosevelt) in a
splendid spirit of calm, judicial reasonableness, and 'Woodrow'
then closed with one of this really masterful speeches. . . . The
final lineup was about as follows, anti-Roosevelt, 5; pro-Roosevelt,
10; undecided, one."

A further conversation I had with Wilson some time afterward
is pertinent to this same discussion. During the month of March,
1911, I was "precepting" in the senior American history course,
and among the texts in use was Wilson's *Division and Reunion*.
One day with several successive sections of students we analyzed
this book to determine from it, if possible, from which side of the
Civil War Wilson wrote. The students decided it was impossible
for them to tell. My reply was that one thing indicated it. Wilson
used the Southern nomenclature for many of the battles, such as
"Manassas" and "Pittsburgh Landing" for the federal names "Bull
Run," "Shiloh," etc. On the seventeenth of the same month, I was
on my way to Philadelphia and Wilson was on the train. I told him
the story, and he remarked that this was the greatest praise he ever
had received for the book. I then asked him pointedly which side
he was on. The following is taken from my diary:

"FRIDAY, MARCH 17, 1911.—Told me *his* views on the secession question. Said South had history and law on her side, since
Constitution did not prohibit secession, and lawyer's principle you
cannot read into a law more than the makers of the law evidently
intended. No questioning of the right of secession until after the

War of 1812. On the other hand, country had developed so that it was a moral crime to attempt to break it up. That particularism cannot be the object of government. Also said that United States Constitution was not a New England product. Only really active New Englander in the Constitutional Convention was Roger Sherman who brought in the Connecticut Compromise."

I also distinctly remember he said that the Constitution was a "Virginia document," and that the nation was in 1789 a confederation which had grown into a unity by 1830, "when Daniel Webster called the Union into being by his reply to Hayne."

Years later, on July 5, 1919, to be exact, my wife and I were lunching with Mr. and Mrs. Moses Taylor Pyne at their home on the outskirts of Princeton. I remember that Mr. Bayard Henry was among the guests, and read aloud a letter he had recently received from Viscount Bryce, this famous British scholar saying, "as for Wilson and the United States Senate, why will he persist in stroking the cat the wrong way?" After lunch we strolled in the garden, Mr. Pyne and I discussing Wilson. Mr. Pyne said that Wilson had once told him that he received a flattering offer to write the life of Thomas Jefferson, but he refused. One day, in the autumn of 1907, I met Wilson on the campus, between Nassau Hall and the entrance to the university library. He stopped and said, "I have just been reading one of the greatest books, sent me by a friend, and by a British shopkeeper of whom I never had heard. The book is the life of Alexander Hamilton, by Frederick Scott Oliver." He went on to describe it. Of course I went at once to the nearby university store and ordered a copy, which I have read a number of times and which I have frequently used as a class text. The influence of this book can be plainly seen upon Wilson, especially after he became President of the United States. The Simmons-Underwood Tariff is in direct line with Oliver's statement of the policies of Hamilton on the tariff. Also, most significantly, the book is extremely critical of Thomas Jefferson.

As president of Princeton Wilson showed those peculiarities of person and character which remained dominant, at least throughout all his later life, both as Governor of New Jersey and President of the United States. He was a man of strong likes and dislikes, and of dominating character. His driving force would brook no opposition. This explains his personal dislike of Theodore Roosevelt, and the dislike was thoroughly reciprocated. These two men were too much alike to get along together without friction. The last time I ever saw Theodore Roosevelt he told me in private conversation and in blistering language his unfavorable opinion of Wilson. And Wilson on many occasions expressed his opinion of Roosevelt. The only time I remember him as being absolutely uncommunicative on the subject of Roosevelt was during the campaign in the primaries for delegates to the national nominating conventions from New Jersey in the spring of 1912. Roosevelt spoke from the balcony of the old Nassau Inn on Nassau Street. Meeting Wilson on Nassau Street, I joined him and we stood together in the crowd in front of the First Presbyterian Church across the street to listen to "Teddy." The latter was completely worn out physically and made the worst speech I ever heard from him. Wilson said not a word, but was the gentleman toward his presumed opponent in the fall election.

But Wilson was an adept in using the steamroller, and never deviated from a course he thought right, or perhaps also advantageous. On one occasion he fell into an argument with a professor of the Princeton Theological Seminary with whom he was playing a friendly game of pool. The argument became so hot that, in order to end what had become dangerous disagreement, the professor remarked, "Well, Dr. Wilson, there are two sides to every question."

"Yes," was the reply, "a right side and a wrong side!"

Furthermore, although Wilson would have been perhaps the last person to realize it, he placed everything upon a personal basis—if it were important to him. If you agreed with him you were perfect; if you disagreed, you were guilty of a personal insult. You were either his friend or his foe. He had great vision, but followed his objectives without too great care about the possibility or the availability of the means to attain them.

There was also a strange duality of personality about the man. In the first place, he could be as cold as a veritable iceberg when he wanted to be. The story was told that on one occasion a student of Princeton fell into difficulties and was about to be expelled. His mother came to plead for him and finally was able to see President Wilson himself, who of course seldom busied himself with the details of such matters. Wilson was obdurate when the woman pleaded and finally she burst into tears and said, "Dr. Wilson, if you expel my son it will kill me!" Wilson replied, "Madam, if it is a question between your life and the life of Princeton University, my mind is made up."

Also he could be vindictive. During the early days in the White House, a younger member of the faculty, as a friend of the Wilson family, was at an informal meal with them when the conversation turned to the subject of the late controversies at Princeton. Wilson remarked bitterly, "I am going to expose the whole thing some time."

In strong contrast to all this, Wilson could show a power of rare fascination, and was then the best of companions and the most sympathetic of friends. He had great gifts of storytelling and a large fund of anecdotes, with a keen sense of humor, provided the matter did not touch him personally. He would, in fact, enjoy telling jokes on himself, but never liked to have them told about him by other people. When he was not personally concerned he could be most generous, helpful, and nonpartisan. But if something did affect him, he could be utterly selfish and even ruthless.

A good illustration of his powers of personal attraction occurred some time around the spring of 1909, when the late Judge Alton B. Parker, who had been recently the Democratic candidate for President of the United States, came to Princeton to give a public lecture. Although I never had met Judge Parker up to that time, in later years I was privileged to know him fairly well, and can speak without reserve of his own personal charm and attraction. He was one of the most charming men I ever met, which makes the following incident all the more significant.

The evening of the judge's lecture I had another engagement, so was unable to hear him, but went later to the Nassau Club where a "smoker" was being given in his honor. I was evidently among the earliest arrivals, and when I went into the club parlor, Judge Parker was standing in a sort of small receiving line, with Mr. Bayard Stockton (the president of the club at that time, I believe) on one side and Mr. George Allison Armour, a leading citizen of Princeton, on the other. I was introduced to the judge, and after a few remarks turned around, and saw Wilson standing alone by a window. He also had evidently just arrived, and had just been introduced. I walked over to him, and was received with that rare cordiality and charming smile he could bestow. I remarked that Hinton R. Helper, of the *Impending Crisis* fame, had just died in a small rooming house in Washington, D.C. Wilson was amazed by the story, and remarked, "What? Hinton R. Helper? That is a voice from the tomb." The conversation went on from one thing to another as others joined us, until at the end of forty-five minutes or an hour I looked around and found that a large crowd was surrounding Wilson and fairly hanging upon his words, although they saw him frequently from day to day. Judge Parker was sitting upon the sofa in the same corner as before, alone with the exception of Mr. Armour and Mr. Stockton.

A charming and memorable occasion is thus described by my diary:

"TUESDAY, APRIL 14, 1908.—This evening our department gave a dinner at the 'Inn' in honor of Harry A. Garfield, who leaves at the end of the year to become President of Williams College. . . . Daniels* presided, and only two set speeches, by Wilson and Garfield. Both splendid. 'Woodrow' 'opened his heart' in an un-

* Winthrop M. Daniels, then Professor of Economics at Princeton [ed.].

usually intimate manner. . . . Afterward we all sat around and told jokes for an hour or two—'Woodrow' leading. A most delightful and successful occasion."

Like most men who enter public life, and especially political life, Wilson had charges of untruthfulness leveled against him from time to time. Without giving any judgment on the question, about which I know but little, there is a possible explanation which should be offered. Herbert Baxter Adams, under whose guidance I was a student at Johns Hopkins from the years 1897 to 1900, once remarked to several of us: "Woodrow Wilson has the worst memory of any man I ever taught. I could have failed him on his examinations if I had asked him questions of fact, but give him something to work out and he was magnificent." In support of this, I may tell of the experience when, during the latter part of January, 1910, I conferred with Wilson at his home in Prospect about some work at Princeton. He finally said, since he was leaving for a Bermuda vacation the next day, "Let us wait until I get back from Bermuda on March 7, and then we can take it up."

He paused a moment, and then added in a whimsical tone of voice and with a twinkle in his eye, "You know what a terrible memory I have?"

My reply was an evasive, "Is that so?"

"Well," he continued, "when I saw by the sailing and arrival of the ship that I should be back on March 7, I at once thought of Daniel Webster's 'seventh of March speech' on the Compromise of 1850!"

Finally, it may be added that you could work *for*, but not always *with*, Wilson. He would be most gracious in his directions and tell you to "do as you think best," but there was always underneath plainly the veiled injunction, "but do it this way." At least that is the way I always felt. He was dominant always, or he was restless and dissatisfied. All these things taken together may help to explain both his great successes and his failures. He had driving power, and pushed ruthlessly ahead.

. . . it is hardly necessary to go into details concerning the most unfortunate controversy at Princeton, but any discussion of Wilson would be incomplete that did not mention it. During the years of his presidency of Princeton he reorganized almost the entire university administration and its curriculum, and also attempted to change the organization and spirit of its life along lines that he considered more democratic. He ran roughshod over old customs and prejudices and was characteristically impatient of opposition. Of course, as is well known, his leading opponent was the able and brilliant dean of the Graduate School, Andrew Fleming West, who proved to be a foeman worthy of his steel, and concerning whom Wilson is reported to have said that in all his career, including the offices of Governor and President, West was the ablest politician he ever met. And West also was a man of charm and great personal attraction. As well stated at the time by a reporter of the *Boston Transcript,* the main differences between the two were in large part due to the fact that Wilson was a Calvinistic Puritan, and West was a Renaissance humanist.

It was early in the controversy that the famous debates occurred in several university faculty meetings during which Wilson made one of the greatest speeches of his career and, to me, probably the greatest speech I ever heard made by anyone. The subject of discussion was fundamentally the attempt to reorganize the social life of the student body. My diary accounts, written immediately after each meeting, may be of some value.

"THURSDAY, SEPTEMBER 26, 1907.—The question of the 'Social Co-ordination of the University'—President Wilson's plan to abolish or transform the upper class clubs—was precipitated in faculty meeting this afternoon. Wilson broached it at commencement time, and it has been agitating faculty, students, and alumni ever since. This afternoon [Winthrop M.] Daniels offered a resolution endorsing the plan and providing for the appointment of a faculty committee to aid the President in carrying it out. Seconded by 'Granny' [Theodore W.] Hunt. Henry van Dyke offered another resolution to throw the whole thing to a joint committee of faculty and trustees for investigation, which everyone looks upon as a veiled hit at 'Woodrow.' Seconded by 'Jack' Hibben and [Howard] McClenahan. The air was electric for a few minutes, but the whole thing has been put over till an adjourned meeting next Monday afternoon. There will be fun then."

"MONDAY, SEPTEMBER 30.—A faculty meeting. Fine debate of two hours. The opposition voted down 81 to 23. Fine speeches by them—Paul van Dyke calling upon Wilson in a frank, sincere speech, and asking him to deal openly with them, and also with the alumni. This called forth from the President one of the most wonderful speeches I have ever heard. I shall never forget him standing there erect behind the desk, the gavel (mallet head) grasped in his right hand, with the end of the handle occasionally placed firm against the top of the desk as he leaned slightly forward in the earnestness of his plea, and his voice occasionally thrilling with an unusual amount of *visible* emotion (for him)— while he stated his dignified position that the faculty must express its opinion without publicly 'investigating' before he could go before the students and alumni in advocacy and explanation of his idea. The whole thing in superb language and diction. A truly wonderful man."

I may add here that when he finished, the faculty actually cheered as well as applauded, and I distinctly remember seeing Dean West, good sport that he was, joining heartily in the applause.

"MONDAY, OCTOBER 21.—Short faculty meeting at four o'clock. As the trustees at their meeting last Wednesday rescinded *their* vote in favor of 'Woodrow's' Quad plan, leaving him permission to go ahead with the agitation of it as an open question, Professor Daniels gave notice of the withdrawal of his motion of approval, to be submitted in another form at the next regular meeting."

Wilson was finally defeated on this question and also upon the main matter at issue with Dean West, the location of the proposed graduate college. However, there is no doubt that he was supported in the main by a majority of both the faculty and the student body. As repeatedly happened in the future, Wilson was extremely, even brilliantly, successful at first in his administration at Princeton, then later seemed to outrun his full usefulness or efficiency. The Democratic nomination for Governor of New Jersey came at a fortunate time for him, for undoubtedly he would have been forced to resign from Princeton within the near future following his defeats in university policy in the year 1910. A little more tact and spirit of compromise, and there might have been a very different story.

There is no doubt that Wilson long had harbored political ambitions and was merely waiting for a propitious time and opportunity to gratify them. This soon became known to other people. If I remember correctly, it was as early as the spring of the year 1907, or certainly in 1908, that the students during their "Senior Singing" had a verse in their "Faculty Song" which ran as follows:

> Here's to Woodrow, King Divine,
> Who rules this place along with Fine,*
> We hear he wants to leave the town
> And try for Teddy Roosevelt's crown.

The nomination of Wilson for the office of Governor of New Jersey on September 15, 1910, by the Democratic party convention was a perfect illustration of effective machine politics and boss rule. In spite of openly expressed protests and strong opposition on the part of some delegates, the bosses had their way and Wilson was nominated by the use of the most highhanded steamroller methods. The convention was held in the Taylor Opera House at Trenton, and Wilson was awaiting the results at Princeton. He was brought over by a hurried automobile trip to Trenton, appeared

* Henry B. Fine, Professor of Mathematics and Dean of the Faculty [ed.].

before the convention and made a very pleasing impression. He accepted the nomination in terms that to a great extent mollified the hostility of some of the delegates and leaders, and soon thereafter he succeeded in arousing the enthusiastic support of the rank and file of the party. Of course he would appeal in addition to the independent voters and also to the less partisan Republicans, and it was upon this support that the Democratic leaders were relying to elect him. They were entirely successful at the ensuing November election.

I called upon Wilson on some matter of university business at Prospect on September 17, the second evening following the convention. I was cordially received and made the remark that I regretted that Dr. Wilson soon would leave Princeton. The reply of the latter was: "You know that for many years I have been preaching to the young men of Princeton that it was their duty to give service to the public and take their part in political affairs. This nomination has been handed to me upon a silver platter and I am under no obligations of any shape, manner, or form to anybody. I hate like poison to leave this place but I could not refuse."

BURTON J. HENDRICK

✪

Governor of New Jersey

Until 1910 the Democratic party in New Jersey had not carried a single state election for seventeen years. There were plenty of reasons for this lack of confidence. The last time the Democratic party had controlled New Jersey, in 1893, it had signalized itself in two ways: by handing the state government bodily over to the racetracks and the railroads, and by electing James Smith, Jr., of Newark, to the United States Senate. Both of these acts had disastrous consequences for New Jersey and the nation. Smith, in Washington, at once became one of that coterie of Democratic Senators, of which other members were Brice and Gorman, who allied themselves with the Republicans, and so prevented that thorough revision of the tariff for which Grover Cleveland had been elected President. In the face of this record, Senator Smith had never lost his absolute control over the Democratic organization in New Jersey. He held this control in spite of the most widespread distrust and unpopularity. Personally, indeed, Smith is not without charm: he is a portly, well-dressed, prosperous figure, with a handsome, smooth, shining face, topped by a mass of well-brushed white hair. He is an Irishman, with all the Irishman's geniality and talent in handling men; able in business, having

From Burton J. Hendrick, "Woodrow Wilson: Political Leader," *McClure's Magazine*, XXXVIII (December 1911), pp. 217–231. Copyright 1911 by *McClure's Magazine*.

accumulated a large fortune through his own efforts; and, as a dispenser of hospitality at his summer home in the Garfield cottage at Elberon, he has easily accumulated a large political and social following. He is a political chieftain of the well-known corporation type, and a man cynically out of touch with the people. Ever since his election to the Senate, he had ruled the New Jersey Democrats by the usual methods—large campaign contributions, reinforced by unquestioned personal masterfulness.

There was only one other man in the state, indeed, who approached Smith anywhere in political power. This was his part-time foe, his part-time friend, "Bob" Davis, the little bowlegged, narrow-browed boss of Hudson County. Davis had not the suavity of Smith; he was a political leader of the traditional Tammany kind. His father, an Irish teamster, had brought him to this country in 1848, when Davis was three years old. He spent all his life in Jersey City. At ten he secured employment as the driver of a hoisting-horse, and a few years later he entered the employ of the gas companies which he was afterward so faithfully to serve in politics. Davis' earlier employment, however, was of a humbler order: he became a "gas-meter measurer," and, in this occupation, he had to go around, from tenement to tenement, measuring the monthly consumption of gas. As a political apprenticeship this experience was almost as useful as keeping a saloon; it brought Davis into personal contact with thousands of poor people, and laid the basis for that wide personal acquaintance without which success of the Tammany kind is impossible. Davis, once started in politics, advanced rapidly. He bought coal for the poor in winter, gave them chowder parties in summer, paid funeral expenses, kept wayward sons out of jail, and generally practiced statesmanship as it is known in large American cities. His political methods, like-wise, were of the Tammany kind: he stuffed ballot boxes, employed "repeaters," exchanged colonizers with Tammany across the river, levied blackmail upon lawbreakers, and incidentally obeyed the orders of the corporations.

Smith, with his nephew "Jim" Nugent, Davis, and a few others, were the Democratic "Overlords," the unassailable masters of the Democratic party in New Jersey. The Republican suzerains were popularly known as the "Board of Guardians." According to the prevailing opinion, the "Overlords" and the "Board of Guardians" really represented one unified political power—a bipartisan machine existing for the purpose of controlling New Jersey in the interests of the corporations. And no state has had quite so disgraceful a corporation record as this one. The railroad and public utility corporations have for many years virtually owned the commonwealth. The bipartisan organization had successfully blocked all popular uprisings. There had been plenty of intelligent public sentiment in New Jersey; the mass of the people were opposed to existing conditions; but, with the exception of a successful outbreak here and there, they had not made much headway. There had been reformers and "new idea" men who demanded new election laws, direct primaries, corrupt practices acts, a public utilities commission, and other "progressive" legislation. For several years bills providing for such laws had been presented to the legislature, only to have their passage invariably stopped by the bipartisan machine. In the Republican state convention of 1910 one of the delegates, George L. Record, New Jersey's most active "progressive," moved to have all these demands included in the Republican platform. He was received with hoots and jeers and general cries of "Put him out!"

In the summer of 1910 the Democratic leaders saw that the party would have a chance to elect a Governor. Should it likewise succeed in electing a Democratic legislature, that would mean a new Democratic Senator. In spite of the fact that Smith's career in the Senate had aroused extremely bitter criticism, he continued to nourish hopes of a return. Here was his opportunity. He and Davis got together to study the best way of accomplishing this result. They decided that the president of Princeton University was by all odds their best play. Smith planned to nominate him for Governor, make use of his great reputation to elect a Democratic legislature, and so climb into the United States Senate over Wilson's back. It was a well-thought-out scheme; but Wilson, schoolmaster that he was, saw through it. Many times Wilson's friends had approached him on the Governorship question; always, however, he had declared that he would participate in no movement that might send Smith back to the Senate.

In the summer of 1910 there was a historic luncheon party at the Lawyers' Club in New York. Several of New Jersey's most influential Democrats there met and talked with President Wilson. They offered to do everything in their power to make him the candidate for Governor. The people thought that Wilson could win, and they offered their services on that ground, specifically declaring that they exacted no conditions and no promises.

"I have a feeling, Doctor, that we are making history today," said Robert S. Hudspeth, the national committeeman from New Jersey. "I think that we are starting a movement that will end by making you President."

"You are looking a long way ahead," laughed Mr. Wilson, and presently he passed to the really important point. If a Democratic legislature were elected, would that mean Smith's return to the Senate? And then he was assured that it would not—that Smith had outgrown that ambition. On these grounds Mr. Wilson agreed to enter the contest.

The campaign had not gone far when New Jersey and the rest of the country perceived that a new type of political leader had arrived. Wilson soon disclosed himself as a man of a type exceedingly rare in our public life—a man with ideas. Most men selected as candidates for Governor, when they are not professional politicians, belong to specialized classes—successful businessmen, lawyers, and the like. These men, excellent as their intentions may be, are sadly handicapped by ignorance; they have no well-thought-out ideas on public affairs, and accept the more or less mechanical standards that prevail. Woodrow Wilson, however, is our profoundest student of public affairs. He had studied administration after administration, state after state—studied them not only in books, but in newspapers, correspondence, and direct contact with men; and, as a result, he had certain definite ideas. If one wishes to grasp the real significance of his work as Governor, one should turn to that little book on "Congressional Government" which he wrote, as a young man, while waiting for clients in his lawyer's office in Atlanta. In this book he puts his finger directly upon the cause of much of the confusion and inefficiency of American public life. That cause is the absence of centralized party leadership.

First and foremost, Mr. Wilson is a strict party man—a man who believes that political parties provide the best possible means for the orderly conduct of public business. In the United States the people have almost automatically divided into two great parties. In view of this fact, thinks Mr. Wilson, it is somewhat unfortunate that our system of government, federal and state, presents so many obstacles to direct party control. It was organized in the days when the classical theory of the separation of the three powers of government—executive, legislative, and judicial—prevailed. We have a complicated system of checks and balances, of executive against legislature, of House against Senate, of Supreme Court against both. In neither our federal nor our state government, therefore, have we any central organized leadership, any authoritative body that can formulate a party program and carry it through directly. An attempt to separate the legislative and executive departments simply destroys all responsible party leadership. We frequently have an executive belonging to one party and a legislature belonging to another; even when the same party controls both branches, the fact that the executive keeps himself separate from the legislature necessarily implies a divided head. In the Governor's office there is one leader; in both the houses of legislation there are others. There is thus no authoritative group that can both propose legislation and carry on administration. It is largely for this reason that American politics has developed an irresponsible leadership. The separation of the powers in the United States is merely a "literary theory"; actually they are identified, though not in the way that makes for efficient government. The political bosses and machines have developed outside of the state constitutions. These agencies have nullified the Constitution and made the executive and legislature one. Thus the boss system does emphatically provide a centralized leadership; but it is irresponsible, unofficial, constantly works in the dark, and inevitably spells gigantic corruption.

Governor Wilson makes no secret of the fact that he admires the British cabinet system. In England the responsible rulers are simply a committee of Parliament, composed of the leaders of the political party which has won the people's confidence at the polls. These leaders control the government in both its executive and legislative branches. They propose and pass needed legislation, and they likewise enforce it. They are hampered by no "checks and balances" they govern directly, with immediate personal responsibility for their success or failure. The one source of their authority is public opinion, and they hold office only so long as the people endorse their acts. Bills are not strangled in committee, as with us; they are openly proposed and debated in full Parliament, and the responsible ministers must be ready at any moment to defend and explain them. Governor Wilson does not believe that this simple system could be advantageously transplanted to this country. He does believe, however, that the American genius will work out some more direct method of transacting public business than now prevails, and substitute some kind of responsible leadership in place of the boss system. This can be done, he thinks, in spite of the fact that we live under rigid, written constitutions. The head and front of this new leadership, according to Mr. Wilson's idea, should be the elected executive. Unquestionably, the American people look for guidance to their President rather than to Congress, just as the states look to their Governors rather than to their legislatures. All the people have had a voice in choosing their executive, only a comparatively few a voice in electing any particular lawmakers. The daily press constantly reflects the greater interest popularly manifested in the executives. The speeches of the President and of Governors are printed in great detail, and arouse the widest discussion; the debates in Congress and the state legislatures receive only the slightest attention. Mr. Wilson, therefore, believes that the Governor of a great state like New Jersey must necessarily assume an active, energetic control. He must take his position as the responsible captain of the party, and become the chief instrument in directing its policies, in both the legislative and executive departments. Fortunately, the Governor can assume this authority without in any degree usurping unconstitutional powers. The constitution of New Jersey, as well as that of most other states, besides giving the Governor a direct veto over legislation, thus virtually making him a third house, specifically says that he shall "recommend measures." If this "recommendation" takes the form of actually presenting drafted bills and using all honorable means to secure their passage, the Governor has not overstepped the powers of his office, even technically.

Early in the campaign Mr. Wilson's opponent struck the usual attitude, and complacently announced that, if elected, he would be a "constitutional Governor." By that he meant that he would live up to the "literary theory" of the separation of the powers; that he would shut himself tightly in the executive chamber, make recommendations, but use no pressure or influence on the legislature. Mr. Wilson at once accepted this challenge. If that was what was meant by being a constitutional Governor, he promised the people that he would be an "unconstitutional Governor." He declared that, if elected, he would regard himself as the leader of his party. He would have his advisers, of course, but he proposed to have an active hand in all the party's policies. He would constantly keep in touch with the members of his party in the legislature, discuss legislation with them, and take part in framing the great party measures. He would not stop at "recommendations," but he would use all honorable means to get the party measures through. He would not do this, however, by bribery—by purchasing support with patronage; his ambition was to bring about "a government by public opinion." He would take the people into his confidence; he would learn what they wanted; he would tell them constantly how things were going on—how particular legislators were serving them, and how others were perhaps betraying them. In other words, he would be their spokesman, their directly chosen representative in the government.

In this way Mr. Wilson would eliminate the rule of the machines. In this he had discovered his cure for the boss system. James Smith, Jr., "Jim" Nugent, "Bob" Davis, and the other chieftains grew somewhat nervous while talk like this was going on. Nor did Wilson leave them long in doubt as to where they personally stood. In the course of the campaign, George L. Record, of Jersey City, addressed a letter to the Democratic candidate, asking definite replies to certain definite questions. On the subject of bosses, Democratic and Republican, Mr. Record's question and Mr. Wilson's answer were as follows:

MR. RECORD. In referring to the Board of Guardians, do you mean such Republican leaders as Baird, Murphy, Kean, and Stokes? Wherein do the relations to the special interests of such leaders differ from the relations to the same interests of such Democratic leaders as Smith, Nugent, and Davis?

MR. WILSON. *I refer to the men you name. They differ from the others in this—that they are in control of the government of the state, while the others are not, and cannot be if the present Democratic ticket is elected.*

Mr. Wilson asked for the suffrages of New Jersey on this explicit issue of his personal leadership. If the people did not desire him to assume control, he particularly asked them not to vote for him. When, therefore, Mr. Wilson was elected on an enormous vote—changing a Republican plurality into a large

Democratic plurality—he at once assumed the responsible chieftainship of the Democratic organization.

The first important test was made upon the election of the new United States Senator. The Democrats had a majority in the legislature, and thus they controlled the Senatorial situation for the first time since 1892. Manifestly this was a matter strictly outside of the Governor's province. The "constitution" gave the legislature the right to elect this Senator; and for the Governor to lift a hand would, under the traditional standards, be "unconstitutional." . . . Not so, however, Governor Wilson. He had become not only Governor, but the leader of the Democratic party, and the selection of a United States Senator was clearly one of that party's greatest responsibilities. In order to assert this authority, however, it was necessary first to sweep away certain obstructions. For the old irresponsible leadership was now once more asserting itself. It found its spokesman in ex-Senator Smith. According to the old political order, Smith had every right to control the party. In Wilson he had elected "his man," and he had also elected "his" Democratic legislature. James Smith was therefore now the party boss. It was his privilege to step forward as head of the organization, to organize the legislature in his own interest, appoint committees, frame legislation, issue orders, dictate appointments, and generally control the executive and legislative departments. True, Mr. Wilson had denounced these things upon the stump; but that, as Smith well understood, was an old-time vote-catching "gag." Of course, the Governor had never really meant it. Smith certainly intended to control the election of United States Senator; furthermore, he proposed to appropriate this great prize for himself. He had been waiting patiently for many years, all the time making large money contributions. Was he not entitled to his reward? A slight obstacle was furnished by the fact that the party voters, at the last party primary, had expressed their preference for Mr. James E. Martine as United States Senator. But Smith believed he could now brush Martine aside.

The Governor-elect, however, had seriously meant everything he had said. He served notice on Smith and Davis that he was the leader of the Democratic party, not they, and that, as leader, he should certainly oppose Smith's election to the Senate. Mr. Wilson went to Newark and Jersey City and served this notice in person. A dramatic meeting took place between Wilson and Smith—the new type of leader and the old; the leader chosen by the suffrages of the people and the leader chosen by all the indirection of machine politics: Wilson tall, scholarly, with a somewhat gaunt and deeply lined Scotch face, as strong and lithe in figure as one of his own Princeton athletes; Smith sleek, well fed, round-faced, suave in manner, insinuating and persuasive in voice.

Wilson informed Smith that he had been given to understand before election that Smith would not be a candidate—that certain domestic afflictions as well as his own health had put him out of the mood for active public life.

"Yes, that's true," replied Smith, smiling; "but I feel better now."

And then Smith told the long story of what he had done for the Democratic party and the money he had contributed to it. Wilson replied that all this was entirely aside from the point—that the point was the matter of keeping faith with the people. Smith then ridiculed Martine for his unfitness, to which Wilson's answer was that, of the fifty-five thousand Democrats who had expressed a preference at the polls, the great majority had endorsed Martine. In fine, Wilson demanded that Smith immediately withdraw his candidacy, and said that he should certainly fight him as effectively as he knew how.

"Yes, and I suppose you'll beat me, Doctor," said Smith. "But you'll do it by using the patronage."

"No, I won't," replied Wilson quickly. "I'll fight you fair. I shall defeat you simply by making use of public opinion."

Leaving Smith, Mr. Wilson now sought out Davis. He found

him in his little red brick house among the plain people—the house from which Davis had for many years ruled the political destinies of Hudson County. Davis was slowly dying of cancer; his face was pinched and white, but his political militancy was still undimmed. He suggested that Wilson keep his hands off the Senatorial situation. "If you do, Governor, we'll support you in your whole legislative program."

"How do I know you will?" replied Wilson, rejecting the proffered "deal." "If you beat me in this the first fight, how do I know you won't be able to beat me in everything?"

Davis laid his hand affectionately upon the shoulder of the ex-president of Princeton. "I've given my word to Smith, Governor. Nothing now can induce me to go back on him."

Wilson now gave the state a typical illustration of the new leadership. Under the old system, the boss summoned members of the legislature to headquarters and delivered his orders. The members of the New Jersey legislature discovered that there was now an "old man" of a different kind. This new centralizing force was not an unofficial person, but the official head of the state. His headquarters were not in a lawyer's office or a bank, but in the shades of Princeton. The Democratic members of the legislature received invitations to spend a few hours at the Governor's house, to discuss the Senatorial situation. They came there in batches of six or eight. They found the new "boss" quite different from the old. He did not order them to do certain things; he did not browbeat: he simply discussed. He said what he thought about the Senatorial contest, and invited expressions of opinion from his guests. He eloquently appealed to his visitors on the basis of party faith. Mr. Wilson offered no rewards; indeed, he told all members distinctly that he would not repay them with patronage. They were Democrats; the Democratic party had made certain pledges to the people; and surely, as Democrats, they would not betray the state? Nor did the Governor threaten the disobedient with punishment;

the nearest he came to this was to suggest that, if any Assemblyman or legislator desired it, he was willing to go into his district
and publicly debate the issue.

"We can't go against that man! We never can face our people
again if we do."

This was the idea with which most of the legislators left the
Governor's presence. The Democratic party in New Jersey, they
felt, had found its leader; and he was guiding it for its own and the
state's good, and not for his own. Mr. Wilson now fortified his
position by redeeming his campaign pledge and taking the stump
against Smith. He went up to Newark, Smith's home town, and
told large and enthusiastic audiences precisely why Smith ought
not to go back to the Senate. His policy demonstrated once more
the enormous force that public opinion exercises in American
public life. In November and December the average observer
would have ridiculed the idea that this Princeton schoolmaster,
by using these direct but simple methods, could have kept "Jim"
Smith out of the United States Senate. Good heavens—hadn't
Smith the votes? Hadn't he been the boss of the party for seventeen years? But, when Mr. Wilson openly entered the fight, all
opposition disappeared. Public pressure became so strong on the
legislators that they fled from Smith in droves. The independent
newspapers took the Governor's side; letters and telegrams rained
in upon Assemblymen and Senators; the Governor's voice had put
the whole state in flame. Martine was elected on the first ballot,
and Smith was unable even to hold all the votes from his own and
Davis' counties.

And in this triumph the Governor accomplished more than the
defeat of Smith: he settled, and settled early in his administration,
an extremely important point. That was the leadership of the
Democratic party in New Jersey. Everybody now understood that
the real leader was the man whom the voters had chosen. Smith
and his coterie might still make trouble—as, indeed, they did—but
their capacity thereafter was limited merely to that of annoyance.

And now Mr. Wilson, as party leader, began the work of framing the party program. Like a prime minister, he selected a body of advisers in the legislature—a number of leading legislators who were to join hands with him in framing bills and getting them made law. The New Jersey legislature was by no means destitute of talent. There were men like Fielder, Osborne, Gebhardt, and Silzer in the Senate: Kenny, Simpson, Egan, and Geran in the House— men who for several years had been specializing in "progressive legislation." There were other political leaders who were not members of the legislature, especially certain newspaper editors who had been for years waging unsuccessful war against the machine. There were others, like Joseph P. Tumulty of Jersey City, a bright young Irishman who had devoted several years to fighting demoralizing tendencies in his own party—and whom Governor Wilson now promptly attached to his staff as private secretary. Here was plenty of valuable material lying fallow; it had made little headway hitherto, simply because it had lacked that dynamic quality which Governor Wilson now gave it—centralized leadership. At the beginning of his term the Governor called these men into counsel. They held an all-day session at the Hotel Martinique in New York, discussing ways and means of obtaining political freedom for New Jersey. These means necessarily took the form of definite legislative proposals. All kinds of laws were discussed. The experiences of other states were gone over; Governor Wilson himself was extensively informed along these lines, and the legislators and the newspaper editors were full of suggestions. Finally, the work was systematized, and different members of the "conference" were assigned to draft bills on particular subjects. In other words, the Democratic party in New Jersey now had a body of men, all under the leadership of Wilson, responsible for the party program and responsive to the public opinion that had placed it in power. It was not a "ministry" or a "cabinet"—it was merely a "conference"; but it served a similar purpose. . . .

It is one of Governor Wilson's favorite ideas that improvement

cannot advance faster than public opinion, and it was his good
fortune to catch this public opinion on the crest. Mr. Wilson
naturally makes no claim to originality for his legislative program.
New Jersey had long been ready for all these reform measures. His
program comprised the changes in our nominating and elective
structure which most observers regard as essential preliminaries to
political change. No one, of course, believes that these new laws in
themselves will destroy the machine system. Only public opinion,
aggressively led, can do that. They merely simplify the machinery
by which this public opinion, once aroused, can effectively express
itself. Clearly, there are certain fundamental abuses that need
correction if this public opinion is to rule. There must, for
example, be an honest ballot. Dead men, men who never existed,
repeaters, colonizers—certainly phantoms of this type should not
be permitted to vote. For years, in New Jersey, vacant lots,
cemeteries, and the circumambient air had contributed largely to
the voting population. The chief measure prepared by the Governor and his "conference"—the so-called Geran Elections Bill—
was intended to correct these evils. Again, a vigilant democracy
has the right to insist that money shall not corruptly influence
elections. Not only shall voters not be purchased directly, but
indirect bribery—cigars, liquor, sale of tickets to entertainments,
promises of office or other favors, campaign subscriptions from
corporations, campaign expenses beyond a certain stipulated
amount, rides to the election booths in automobiles and carriages
—these things likewise must be prohibited. The Governor and his
associates, therefore, prepared a corrupt practices act as rigid as
the famous English law. Above everything else, the party voters
must have a direct hand in nominating men for office. The time has
gone by when "slates" can be fixed up in the back room of saloons
and "slipped through" certain so-called political conventions. An
essential part of the legislative program was therefore a direct
primary—a bill that made the old-time political conventions illegal
and placed the nomination of candidates for all offices, even

United States Senators and delegates to national party conventions, directly in the hands of the party voters.

In the hope of remedying our greatest political abscess, the government of cities, a bill was decided on that would give all municipalities the option of adopting the commission plan of government. The Des Moines plan, which includes the initiative and referendum and the recall, was adopted. And then there was the pressing problem of the corporations. Governor Wilson is not a corporation baiter. He thoroughly believes in corporations, and in their rights. He wishes to see them go on doing their great work—serving the people, paying their bondholders, and earning handsome dividends for their stockholders. He believes, however, that the federal and state governments must exercise a vigilant and definite control; that they should supervise security issues, so that there shall be no repetition of the crimes of overcapitalization; that they shall regulate equipment and service, so that the purpose for which the railroads really exist may be served; finally, that the state shall have the power even to fix rates, so that passengers and shippers shall be protected against extortion. He would apply these principles not only to railroads, but to all corporations that operate under special franchises—trolley lines, gas- and electric-light companies, telephone and telegraph companies, and the like. A public utilities bill was thus another outcome of the Governor's "conference." And then there was the saddest fact of corporation management—the killing and maiming of employees, and the antique laws that prevent the widows and children from obtaining compensation. The last great measure upon which the Governor pinned the success of his administration was, therefore, a fair and honest employers' liability and compensation act. This not only swept away all the legal cobwebs that have defeated justice for nearly a hundred years, but provided a regular scale of compensation which became automatically operative on proof of injury. Under this, if a corporation so injures an employee that he is unable to work, it must make regular substantial weekly contributions to his support. It must pay so much for the destruction of a thumb, a finger, a great toe, "other toes," an arm, a leg, an eye, and so on. If the injuries result in death, the corporation must pay the doctors' bills and funeral expenses and certain graduated weekly stipends to the widow and children for a period of three hundred weeks.

The Governor's "ministry" prepared all these bills, in constant consultation with the Governor himself. Night after night thay met in the executive chamber at Trenton. When all his associates had gone, Mr. Wilson himself would sit bending over his desk far into the early hours of the morning, rewriting here, and correcting there. There are copies of all the bills in existence, bewilderingly smudged with the Governor's own interlineations. In spite of the great work involved, they were all introduced early in the session. The Governor got them in at an early date, so that there might be plenty of time for publicity—for discussion and amendment. He wanted, he told his associates, the advice of every interested person in the state. On the evening when the bills were introduced, Mr. Wilson sat musingly at his desk in the Governor's room. There was no one else present except his secretary, Mr. Tumulty. The bills just placed before the legislature meant, if they were passed, a revolution in the political machinery of the state. Year after year they had come up, in one form or another, only to be stifled by the lobby. And now the same old lobby was gathering strength for its death grapple.

"Do you think the bills will pass, Tumulty?" the Governor asked.

The secretary merely smiled.

"Why do you smile?"

"Because I have been in the legislature for four sessions, and you haven't."

The Governor turned around and began buttoning up his coat— always a sign, with him, of a serious and determined mood.

"They will pass," he said quietly. "They've got to. The people have demanded them. The people will get them in spite of any legislature. The legislature won't dare to turn them down."

And now the state of New Jersey had an entirely new experience in practical methods of legislation. The old way in this state was essentially the same as that which prevails in nearly all others. The laws originated in various unofficial places—in the offices of corporation lawyers or in similarly interested quarters. Once drawn up in their final form, they were handed to the "Big Boss," who, in turn, gave them to his lieutenants for introduction. The "Big Boss" haunted the Capitol during the legislative session; though never a member, he commonly took his station on the floor and personally conducted operations; even in recent years, he has been known to stand directly back of the Speaker and vicariously run the legislative machine. All mere members he treated as just so many slaves. When the time came for a particularly favored bill to pass, the Boss would summon his lieutenants. "Number 164 is up at ten o'clock," he would shout. "Come, line up your men." And then the sub-bosses would go scurrying over the building, dragging forth the lawmakers in batches of four and five. "Get into line; go in and vote for 164," they would command. Few of the legislators had the slightest inkling of what the bill was about; their only business was to do precisely what the "old man" said. Occasionally the Governor would take a hand. He would not send for the members and reason with them; he would merely send them explicit orders. Sometimes, if the situation required it, he would hold forth inducements of an appointment, or he would threaten to veto certain much-desired legislation, should the member prove obdurate. Legislation, therefore, was accomplished either by the direct use of the lash or by bribery and executive blackmail.

This was not Governor Wilson's way. His basic idea was that there existed a Democratic party organization, of which he himself was the head. The leaders of this organization, under his guidance, had adopted a certain legislative program—a program which was intended to redeem the promises made to the people. It was his duty, as party leader, to use all honorable means to get these measures enacted. There was no way in which he could exert pressure, except by personal appeals to the members and to the public. And he did this with a persuasive tact that aroused the enthusiasm of the old-timers. For the whole legislative session the legislators were encouraged to make their headquarters in the Governor's room. He became personally acquainted with them, discussed constantly the pending legislation, and tactfully asked their advice as to possible improvements. He persuaded, he reasoned, he argued, he asked and answered questions. The secret of his power and influence was that he treated his party associates as men and equals. He never promised a thing as a reward; he simply appealed to their party loyalty. The powerful hold he obtained in this way was strikingly shown in the case of an Assemblyman from Mercer County. This man was a modest employee, at about eighteen dollars a week, of a large manufacturing plant located at Trenton. The officers of this corporation evidently believed that, since this man was one of their employees, they had a right to control his action as a legislator. In the Senatorial fight its officers commanded him to cast his vote for Smith. Left to himself, the man would not have hesitated in voting against Smith; but the bread and butter of his wife and children was directly involved.

Many legislators got in the habit of taking their personal troubles to the Governor; and this member now asked Mr. Wilson's advice. "I am afraid I can't advise you," said Wilson. "I appreciate your troubles, and think that I have no right to ask you to sacrifice your family's support. You must settle the question yourself; but, if you vote for Mr. Smith, I shall not hold it against you, as I shall understand your position."

The Assemblyman defied his employers and voted against Smith. He was immediately reduced in employment and put upon "piecework," which meant a reduction in wages to about ten dollars a week. When the matter of the Governor's legislative program came up, this same Assemblyman again received his orders from his employers to vote against it. Once more he appealed to Mr. Wilson, and received the same answer as before. Again he defied the corporation upon which he was dependent for his ten dollars a week. This time he was summarily discharged. The interesting part of this story is that this Assemblyman was not a man who had hitherto shown any marked independence. He was, indeed, of the most ordinary caliber. It was clearly the Governor's influence that had injected certain heroic qualities into him, and the episode is chiefly interesting as indicating the new spirit that had entered the legislature. It is comforting to add, however, that the Assemblyman did not suffer, for an outraged community quickly provided him with employment.

Mr. Wilson made himself accessible not only to members of the legislature, but to all citizens. The best way to settle differences, he believed, was calmly to sit down and talk things over. At first the labor leaders felt somewhat hostile because of the employers' liability bill. They had their own measure, which they regarded as a better one than that which was pushed by the administration. The labor leader having the matter in charge spent some time fuming and denouncing Mr. Wilson, until finally someone suggested that he drop into the executive office and have the matter out. After spending an hour or so with Mr. Wilson, he came out in a high state of enthusiasm. "Why, he's the greatest man in the country!" he exclaimed. "He's dead right, too. He went into the whole matter and showed me just why his bill was a better one than ours. I'm strong for it now."

Still the old lobby, although shorn of nearly all its influence, kept buzzing around. Smith, the owner of two newspapers in Newark, used them chiefly as agents for attacking the Governor and his policies. Wilson, of course, was an "ingrate"; Smith had worked hard to elect him, and now he was using his power to destroy all the things for which the Smith regime had stood. Smith's nephew "Jim" Nugent, the chairman of the Democratic

State Committee, kept hanging about Trenton and the legislature, working here and there against the reform measures. The test came on the Geran Election Bill. The old-timers, as a means of defeating this, demanded a caucus. Someone repeated this to the Governor. "All right," he said; "go on. Why not invite me to the caucus? It's unprecedented, I know. Perhaps it's even unconstitutional; but then, I'm an unconstitutional Governor."

This certainly was an amazing idea. A Governor in a party caucus? And yet, according to Wilsonian principles, why not? Was he not the generally acknowledged leader of his party? Was he not daily exercising all the authority of the party leadership? Why, then, should the party members gather to map out a party program without their chief? There was certainly no one so qualified to shed light upon the difficult points of the measure as the man who had had the leading influence in drafting it.

Somewhat dazed by the proposition, the Democratic members agreed, and the Governor promptly appeared. There was a minority that sullenly rebelled against his presence. Hardly had the Governor begun to talk, when someone interrupted. He bluntly told Mr. Wilson that he had no business in the caucus. What "constitutional" right had the Governor to interfere in legislation, anyway? His duties were of an entirely different "constitutional" kind.

"Since you appeal to the constitution," replied Mr. Wilson, "I think I can satisfy you." And he drew from his pocket a copy of the New Jersey constitution and read the following clause:

The Governor shall communicate by message to the legislature at the opening of each session, and at such other times as he may deem necessary, the condition of the State, and *recommend such measures as he may deem expedient.*

Naturally, that silenced all protests of this kind. The submerged reactionaries, however, were far from cordial in the early stage of the discussion. They accused the Governor to his face of "playing"

for the Presidency—a charge, however, that did not greatly disturb
him. He wished rather to limit his attention to the merits of the
particular bill under consideration. For three hours the Governor
stood there, explaining the bill in detail to his party associates. He
took it up clause by clause, rehearsed the experience of other
states along similar lines, seemed, indeed, to have the political
history of every cranny of the United States at his finger tips.
"Where did this schoolmaster learn so much about politics?" the
legislators asked themselves—"not only legislation, but practical
politics?" After his explanation Mr. Wilson was submitted to a
steady fire of questions. In answering these, he acted like a small
boy playing his favorite game; he certainly enjoyed the proceeding
to the full.

At the conclusion the Governor launched into an impromptu
appeal for support. The eloquence of which he is so great a master
now shone at its best. Several of the legislators present have
described this experience to the writer. "I have never known
anything like that speech," said one. "Such beautiful Saxon English, such suppressed emotion, such direct personal appeal—it was
all wonderful, simply wonderful. The Governor talked for at least
an hour, his speech flowing smoothly, readily, never pausing for a
word or an idea. It was like listening to music. And the whole
thing was merely an appeal to our better unselfish natures. The
state had trusted us, as Democrats, with great duties and responsibilities. Would we betray the people or would we seize this
splendid opportunity? But it is useless to attempt to describe the
speech or the effect that it produced. We all came out of that room
with one conviction, that we had heard the most wonderful speech
of our lives, and that Governor Wilson was a great man. Even the
most hardened of the old-time legislative hacks said that. It has
been said that debate no longer accomplishes anything in American legislation, that nobody is now persuaded by talk. Here was a
case, however, which refutes this idea. When we went into that
caucus we had no assurance as to what the result would be. But

opposition melted away under the Governor's influence. That caucus settled the fate of the Geran bill, as well as the whole Democratic program."

That Mr. Wilson could use other methods than appeal and persuasion, however, was shown by another episode connected with this same election bill. Nugent, the chairman of the Democratic State Committee, the representative of the old type of political leader, kept constantly upon the flanks of the legislature, vainly attempting to club the members into opposing the Governor's program. Someone asked Wilson if he would meet Nugent and talk the matter over. "I will talk things over with any citizen who wishes to see me," said Mr. Wilson. Nugent presently came in—not, however, in a conciliatory mood.

"Don't you think, Mr. Nugent," began the Governor, "that you are making a mistake in opposing this bill?"

"No," said Nugent; "and I don't think you could pass it without using these methods."

"What methods?"

"I mean that you are using patronage."

According to Governor Wilson's ideas, that simply amounted to an accusation of using bribery and blackmail, and he met the charge in the only possible way. He rose to the full height of his six feet, swept his arm in the direction of the door, and said:

"Good day, Mr. Nugent, good day!"

"You're no gentleman," shouted the Boss, as he retreated through the door.

"I don't think you're any judge," replied the Governor, sitting down again and applying himself to his work.

The Boss's face, say those who saw him as he came tearing down the corridor, was almost apoplectic with rage. Consider for a moment who he was—this man whom the Governor had almost bodily "fired" out of his office. As chairman of the Democratic State Committee, as nephew and personal representative of ex-Senator "Jim" Smith, Nugent was the regular accredited state "boss." Had Mayor Van Wyck of New York thrown Richard Croker out on the sidewalk, had Governor Dix ordered Charles F. Murphy from his presence in the course of the Senatorial fight last winter, had President McKinley kicked Mark Hanna out of the White House, they would have pursued exactly the same policy as did Governor Wilson in ejecting Nugent. This, however, was not the main significance of the Governor's act. The episode simply emphasized the fact that men of Nugent's type have absolutely no place in a political organization, as Governor Wilson understands it. A political leader, according to his conception, must be a responsible leader. He must hold office, and he must have been elected by the rank and file of his party. This fact makes him responsible to public opinion, in which he finds his only lease of power. Manifestly Nugent did not fulfill these requirements. In the next few weeks Governor Wilson was able to show that the state of New Jersey and the Democratic party could get along with its responsible leaders without calling in the assistance of its Nugents. In fact, under the new system, Nugent found himself entirely without influence. He made many frantic attempts to "line up his men"; he laid hold of Assemblyman after Assemblyman and almost tearfully pleaded with them to vote against the Governor's bill. The Democratic Assemblymen, however, ignored his appeals. They passed the entire legislative program by a large majority. Even the Senate, which was overwhelmingly Republican, apparently caught the infection, for it quietly endorsed everything the Democratic Governor had asked for.

And so, as a result of the assertion of real leadership by a Governor of great intelligence and force, there must be recorded a real miracle in politics: New Jersey is a "progressive" state. Its legislation is as far "advanced" as that of Oregon, California, and other Western commonwealths. But it is progressive not only in measures, but in methods. Governor Wilson's real service is that he has dissipated a great American governmental superstition: the idea that political parties should work under a divided leadership;

that a Governor, elected by public opinion on certain definite issues, should divorce himself from public opinion and those issues immediately on assuming office. He has shown the necessity of uniting, under centralized party control, both the executive and legislative branches, and has proved that, once such a centralization is established, the power of the boss system disappears. That is Mr. Wilson's great contribution to the solution of our political problems.

✪

A Personal Glimpse

My official connection with Mr. Wilson was almost accidental, though, as I look back over the long stretch of years, I should like to call it providential. After the official luncheon on March 4, 1913, Mr. Wilson's sister, Mrs. Annie Howe, fell on one of the marble staircases and cut her brow. As I was present as a guest and had my equipment handy, I sewed up the wound and attended her for a few days thereafter. The President commented on how promptly it was done and wanted to know if I was prepared for the operation before the accident occurred.

Mr. Wilson asked me to lunch one day, when one of the other guests was the Secretary of the Navy, Mr. Josephus Daniels. To my surprise Mr. Wilson turned to the Secretary and said: "There is one part of the Navy that I want to appropriate. There have been a good many applications for the position but Mrs. Wilson and I have already become acquainted with Dr. Grayson and we have decided that he is the man we should like to have assigned to the White House." To which Secretary Daniels replied jokingly: "You generally have to come to the Navy when you want a good thing." That is all there is to the story. No official action was necessary because I had already been assigned to the White House during the Taft administration and the assignment was simply continued.

A few days later, on a Sunday morning, I was called into professional attendance upon the President. When I entered the sickroom, Mrs. Wilson, who was standing by the bed, greeted me with her gracious smile. I found the patient lying in bed suffering from a headache and digestive disturbance, which he described as a "turmoil in Central America." He said: "When you get to know me better, you will find that I am subject to disturbances in the equatorial regions." My first professional advice was an injunction to remain in bed, in reply to which he said: "You are advising a new President, and you are giving him bad advice, for you are telling him not to go to church."

This was the beginning of my diagnosis of his general condition and my systematic treatment which depended very little upon drugs. Indeed, when I took his medicines away from him he accused me of being a "therapeutic nihilist." It seemed to me a clear case for preventive medicine. I was able to get his cooperation in my plans through a simple appeal to his reason. I reminded him that he had four hard years ahead of him and that he owed it to himself and the American people to get into as fit condition as possible and to stay there. The regime included plenty of fresh air, a diet suited to his idiosyncrasies as I discovered them by close study, plenty of sleep, daily motor rides, occasional trips on the *Mayflower,* and especially regular games of golf, together with treatment for a persistent case of neuritis from which he had long suffered.

By reason of his outdoor recreation and exercise, I was quickly drawn into close, personal association with him, for I was his regular companion in these diversions. I learned to know something of his habits of mind and his sense of humor, which, by the way, was one of the things that assisted much in enabling me to keep him in good condition.

It was the second day of his first illness that he told me some of his characteristic anecdotes. He told me of Dr. Delafield, the New York specialist, an admirable physician but without much sense of humor, who, when he started first to wash out Mr. Wilson's stomach, stood before him with a long rubber tube in his hand and said in a very serious manner: "You will find this extremely disagreeable but not intolerable."

I soon learned that it was easy to get to know Mr. Wilson—if he happened to take a fancy to you. Contrary to widespread opinion, he was not temperamentally cold. He was austere in his public relationships. He would not allow friendship to influence his course of duty. Several years later he told me that if he had a son who was convicted on a criminal charge, and whose case should come before him as chief executive, he would confirm the judgment of the court and then die of a broken heart. . . .

Woodrow Wilson was never afraid of being misunderstood when a principle which he held inviolable was involved. He was not callous. He was sensitive as literary men usually are. In his address at the services held in the Brooklyn Navy Yard in memory of those who lost their lives in the expedition to Vera Cruz in 1914, there occurred this significant passage:

I never went into battle; I was never under fire; but I fancy that there are some things just as hard to do as to go under fire. I fancy that it is just as hard to do your duty when men are sneering at you as when they are shooting at you. When they shoot at you, they can only take your natural life; when they sneer at you, they can wound your living heart, and men who are brave enough, steadfast enough, steady in their principles enough, to go about their duty with regard to their fellow-men, no matter whether there are hisses or cheers . . . are men for a nation to be proud of. . . . The cheers of the moment are not what a man ought to think about, but the verdict of his conscience and of the consciences of mankind.

Consciously or unconsciously Woodrow Wilson made there a better analysis of his motives for action than anybody else can make. He was sincere in his principles, and he had the courage to

stand for them in the face of all consequences. He broke with some
of his friends, and the breaks hurt him, but these severances were
due to differences on some matter of principle. He was impersonal
in the sense that he would not and could not allow a friendship to
stand between him and what he conceived to be his public duty.

Much has been written and will be written about his quarrels,
and it has sometimes been asserted that he had no personal
friends. They who say this ignore the record. For many old
Princeton classmates and collegemates he kept a romantic affection to the end of his life. There was Cyrus McCormick, Cleveland
Dodge, Robert Bridges, E. P. Davis, Edward Sheldon, Charles
Talcott, the brothers Thomas and David Jones. There were associ-
ates in the Princeton faculty like Harry Fine. John Westcott,
George Harper, Winthrop Daniels, Edward Capps. There were
political associates, including members of his Cabinet, between
whom and him there was not only no break in official relationships, but an affection which endured to his life's end: Newton
Baker, Josephus Daniels, Thomas W. Gregory, David F. Houston,
Carter Glass, William B. Wilson. There were many members of
Congress, including John Sharp Williams, Claude A. Swanson,
Cordell Hull, Finis Garrett. There were men whom he had
appointed to diplomatic positions, like Thomas Nelson Page,
Henry Morgenthau, Roland S. Morris, Pleasant Stovall (a school-
boy friend), and Charles R. Crane. There were members of special
war agencies, such as Norman Davis, Bernard Baruch, Frank L.
Polk, Vance McCormick, Jesse H. Jones.

These are merely outstanding figures among many for whom
Mr. Wilson retained to the end a warm, positive friendship. Many
of them were frequent visitors to the house in S Street throughout
the period of Mr. Wilson's retirement. They called unostentatiously, unofficially, as personal friends. . . .

His approach to most public men was courteous but not often
familiar, and yet no one knew better how to lighten a serious
interview with humorous repartee or anecdote. He was by nature

dignified but assumed no artificial dignity. He told me with glee how in the Gubernatorial campaign in New Jersey an old farmer slapped him on the back at the conclusion of a speech, and said: "Doc, you are all right." The President added: "I knew then that I had arrived as a politician."

He was impatient with pompous people and intolerant of those who sought special favors from the government. And because he cherished privacy more than display, he gave his full confidence to comparatively few, and those chiefly of his own household, of which it was my good fortune to become promptly an adopted member.

I think he appreciated the fact that I consistently refused pressure from outside to be a go-between, and that I confined my advice to matters of health, to which he listened attentively and followed unquestioningly. He did me the honor to assume that I knew what I was talking about, and, therefore, did not argue with me. . . .

My personal acquaintanceship and friendship with Mr. Wilson grew simultaneously with my professional knowledge of his physical constitution. He often expressed to me his views as one muses aloud, finding in me a safety valve.

He was never happier than in the bosom of his family, sitting before the fireplace in the Oval Room with us, chatting comfortably. Sometimes his conversation was playful, at other times serious. He would pun, recite nonsense verse and limericks, and then suddenly turn from merriment to gravity, frequently referring to or reading some passage from Burke or Bagehot, from which he would be likely to pass to an essay by Charles Lamb, or Birrell, or Chesterton (in whose glittering paradoxes he found expressed a good deal of his own philosophy of progressive conservatism), or to one of the poets whom he loved, Wordsworth (his favorite), or Browning (a few of whose poems he cherished deeply), or to the poetry of Matthew Arnold, for whose prose he did not care very much.

He was fond of reading aloud in modulated tones from his favorite authors. On the library table close at hand for reference was a copy of Burton Stevenson's large anthology of verse, from which he would sometimes read John Burroughs' poem "Waiting," finding in it perhaps a philosophy of his own life. "For, lo! my own shall come to me," as it did come before his death, after all the fluctuations of rejection and acceptance by the world's opinion. Then from the same book he would read from Lear's nonsense verse and W. S. Gilbert's swinging lyrics—he was especially fond of the Duke of Plaza-Tora.

Occasionally he and his daughter Margaret would sing together a varied repertoire: sometimes old-fashioned Southern songs, sometimes lyrics of Gilbert, or "Old Nassau," the Princeton song, and, especially on Sunday evenings, some of his favorite hymns— "The Day is Dying in the West," "The Son of God Goes Forth to War," "How Firm a Foundation," "The Strife of Life Is O'er."

He had no craving for novelty but liked to do the same thing over and over again. He reread the same books, repeated the same automobile rides, as also, before he came into the Presidency, he revisited many times the English lake country, which he preferred to other parts of Great Britain or to the European continent.

He had strong attachments for articles of long association. He was particularly fond of an old cape and an old gray sweater, which he had purchased in Scotland on one of his bicycling tours in his young manhood, and to which he clung to the end of his life. Handsome sweaters were sent to him as presents, and occasionally he would wear one of them, but would invariably return to his old friend, the Scottish gray sweater with a moth hole in it. It traveled with him wherever he went. It was part of his luggage in Buckingham Palace, in the Quirinal, in the Royal Palace in Brussels. When he was ill in the White House he wore it in bed on all occasions, even when he received the King and Queen of the Belgians and the Prince of Wales. He wore it on his last automobile ride.

In a similar way he clung to a favorite walking stick. He had literally hundreds of canes, some of them purchased when he was a young man, many more of them given to him by friends and admirers after he had become famous. But after he was stricken, he selected one which he always referred to as his "third leg," and he would use no other.

He was pre-eminently a man of habit—of good habits. He had been taught in childhood not to take more food on his plate than he wanted to eat, and this became a lifelong practice. Once when I remarked on this habit of his, he laughingly said that it was part of his thrifty Scotch training.

He always attended Sunday morning service at the Central Presbyterian Church, located when he came to Washington at Third and I streets, Northwest, and subsequently removed to a new building at Sixteenth and Irving streets. He made an address at the laying of the foundation stone of the new edifice, and he and his wife had a keen satisfaction in watching the progress of the building, of which the Reverend Dr. James H. Taylor was pastor.

Mr. Wilson was a lover of sermons if they were sincere and thoughtful, and often as he would ride down Sixteenth Street from the church he would express his admiration for the way in which Dr. Taylor had developed his subject.

It was characteristic of the President to unite with a modest congregation rather than with one of the more fashionable Presbyterian churches of Washington.

He attended church as unostentatiously as the most humble worshipers in the capital. He was the son of a Presbyterian preacher and went to church in the spirit of worship and not for display. He could not have been distinguished from any other devout churchgoer except for the facts that he rode in a car blazoned with the President's seal and was followed, as the law required, by secret service men.

When the war began and his family had grown smaller (Miss Jessie had married Mr. Sayre and moved to New England, Miss

Eleanor had married Mr. McAdoo and united with another church), there was usually room in his pew for others, and Mr. Wilson requested that doughboys occupy the pew with him.

He joined reverently in the prayers and heartily in the singing of the hymns, sometimes sharing his hymnbook with a stranger, sometimes crossing the aisle to give it to others. Knowing most of the hymns by memory he was able to continue singing without the book.

Once he absented himself from state duties to attend a meeting of the presbytery in the Central Presbyterian Church, where he made an address, speaking with authority because he was a ruling elder in the Presbyterian Church.

Wherever he was he attended divine services—in whatever town he might be spending a Sunday on one of his official trips, in Cornish, New Hampshire, and at Shadow Lawn in New Jersey (where he took the brief vacations he had during his terms as President), on shipboard, and at the Paris Conference. . . .

Apology is unnecessary for detailed accounts of Mr. Wilson's relationship with the church, because religion was flesh of his flesh and bone of his bone. He kept the faith which he inherited from his forefathers. He was deeply religious outside of church and on weekdays, as well as inside and on Sundays.

Though he loved anecdotes, he shrank away from any that carried the slightest suggestion of sacrilege. In the first year of daylight saving time, someone repeated in his presence the story of the old Virginia cook who was told to have dinner ready at seven o'clock, and answered irritably: "By what time—Wilson's time or Christ's time?" Everybody in the group laughed, and for a moment Mr. Wilson's own face broke into a smile over the absurdity, but he quickly strangled the smile and remarked: "That is irreverent."

He was no maudlin pietist. He was too much a man for that, and he could laugh, as did his preacher father, at anecdotes about preachers.

He was fond of repeating one of his father's stories of a Scotch dominie who prayed at length, giving the Lord much information, and concluded with: "And Oh Lord, there is much more of this matter, as Thou hast doubtless read in the last number of the Edinburgh *Review.*"

A President at Work

Woodrow Wilson is in the White House.

He is the same man as he who a few weeks ago was sitting in his rooms at the back of the New Jersey State Capitol—the same man, at the same sort of work, with the same manners and methods. He wears the same gray suit, or another off the same piece, built by the same tailor. There is a new stickpin in his tie; he has exchanged the seal of the Union for that of his old state; but if the tie is new, it is an amazing match for the old ones. Pince-nez eyeglass, pencil and notebook, still perform their offices.

The President has already made some new acquaintances, a few thousands; but he hasn't forgotten anyone the Governor ever knew. The President's secretary still calls him "Governor," and probably always will; it is a most happy and fortunate thing that Mr. Joseph P. Tumulty has come along to Washington; and he has brought his two best Trenton stenographers with him. There were three days—a Saturday afternoon, a Sunday, a Monday, and a Tuesday morning—when Mr. Wilson rested, as a private citizen, but that was not long enough to allow him to forget his old ways of work. At nine o'clock on the morning of the fourth day he was

From William Bayard Hale, "Watching President Wilson at Work," *World's Work*, XXVI (May 1913), pp. 69–77. Copyright 1913 by *World's Work*; reprinted by permission of William Harlan Hale.

employing them again as if there had been no interruption, though the scene was slightly altered.

The building in which the head of a nation meets his counselors, directs his officers, puts his signature on papers of state, the building from which go forth the commands of a nation, is the one-storied staff annex to the White House which, to all official intents and purposes, is the White House. Looking at the plan of the place, you get the impression of a puzzle. These offices were devised, you suspect, to keep people away from the President—who can be reached only after threading a labyrinth of chambers and corridors. Until Mr. Wilson came down it was a difficult and hazardous feat to get into the inmost sanctum. Ordinary visitors, after passing the scrutiny of policemen in uniform outside the door and secret service men in mufti just within it, were steered into one waiting room; persons like Senators and Representatives, into another. It was as difficult to get into the office of the Secretary to the President as it is today to get into the President's own room. Doorkeepers moved mysteriously about, beckoning now to this fortunate one, now to that one. And when he was at last admitted to the Presidential presence, the caller found himself only one of four or five or possibly twenty men lining the walls of an oval room, around which the President passed, listening and replying to a few rapid, low-spoken words from each—the room being, by the way, a whispering gallery in which no muttered secret was safe.

Today, the general waiting room is abandoned, and the Congressional room is occupied by stenographers. Visitors who know the way walk unchecked through the lobby and the corridors into the secretary's room. Such as are unfamiliar with the lay of the land may be directed to take a seat somewhere in a lobby until their cards are carried in to Mr. Tumulty; they themselves usually follow promptly. The secretary's room has become the waiting room.

To tell the truth, it is just as hard to get to the President as ever it was. Doubtless anyone so minded could walk straight on through the short hall that leads to the Oval Room and confront the President—but, of course, nobody does that. The doors stand open, and those who reach the desk of the secretary hear the voices of the chief magistrate and his interlocutor, but everybody pauses in the anteroom and waits his special invitation—if one is forthcoming.

The secretary's office is always a scene of lively interest. Mr. Tumulty has an hour to himself in the morning; he is the earliest riser in official life Washington has ever known, and he has been over his mail by the time the first callers begin to arrive. The President likewise has been at work with his stenographer for an hour or two before the first appointments begin, say at ten o'clock. At that time the secretary's room is filled, and it continues to be filled until after one o'clock. An enumeration, at any moment during the morning, of the men, numbering from a dozen to twenty or thirty, to be found there waiting their turns, would be a list practically every name of which would be recognized as that of a national person. At any moment you may be speaking to a cabinet minister, rubbing elbows with three or four Senators, stepping on the toes of a Supreme Court Justice, or knocking against an army officer of high degree.

The rule is that no visitor may see the President without an appointment previously made. A list of expected visitors, every one of whom is assigned a period of from two to twenty minutes, is prepared the first thing in the morning. The program is carried out almost with the accuracy of a railroad timetable. By twelve o'clock the morning's work may possibly be ten minutes behind the schedule; it generally finishes pretty promptly on time, not infrequently with a few spare minutes into which to crowd an additional interview or two. There may be, there generally are, four or five visitors, probably of distinction, who have called without appointment, and who wait, hoping that an opportunity may come by chance to whisper the word they are anxious should reach the President's ear. Such opportunities rarely come. Occasionally the

President steps out of his room and makes a hasty round of the outer office, but these occasions are few, and Washington officials are coming to understand that while they may see the President's secretary at any moment, it is only by appointment previously made that they have much prospect of getting a word with Mr. Wilson himself.

That is to say, during the morning; and by universal consent morning is the time devoted to making and receiving official calls. President Roosevelt and President Taft used to keep open half an hour between noon and twelve thirty for a sort of general reception when those who were without appointments could shake the President's hand and have his ear for a brief moment or two. Mr. Wilson has done away with this custom; in place of it, visitors without appointments are instructed to repair to the East Room of the White House at two thirty, where they pass rapidly before the President and have a brief opportunity for conversation, though, of course, not in private.

Seated in a corner are a group of Senators—Lodge, Smoot, and Stone—waiting for five minutes in which to intercede for a discharged customs official, Judge Sharretts, who was lately removed from office by President Taft and whose friends think President Wilson should reopen his case.

Over by the mantel is a nervous Congressman from Long Island. Equally nervous is a Wisconsin statesman, or statesman-to-be—Mr. "Joe" Davies, who has a handsome profile; he is talking with another, *the* other, specimen of Democratic pulchritude—Mr. A. Mitchell Palmer; the Pennsylvanian is as big and fair as the Wisconsin man is delicate and black.

Enters Joseph Gurney Cannon, the irrepressible, with his carnation in his buttonhole, radiating benevolence and biblical quotations. "I have been advised," he begins cheerfully—"Uncle Joe" is actually going home, after thirty-eight years in Congress—"I have been advised that it is time I made my peace with God. Well, I am afraid I couldn't get an audience with the Almighty, but I can at least hope to see the President. He may have some influence at the throne of grace." The ex-Speaker holds his own little court in the midst of the room, quizzed by Senators and cabinet members.

Here is an anxious politician from Porto Rico. Here is Mr. Pleasant Stovall, an old playmate of Mr. Wilson's, whom the Senators and Congressmen of Georgia unite in recommending for the legation in Switzerland. The blind Senator from Oklahoma, Mr. Gore, has an early appointment for which he is promptly on hand.

Mr. Montague, of Virginia, has been waiting two hours, as yesterday he waited, hoping for a chance to reach the President with the representations which the Progressive Democrats of the Old Dominion are anxious Mr. Wilson should consider before he decides between Mr. Thomas Nelson Page and Colonel Joseph E. Willard for a foreign mission. The Page-Willard fight is preliminary to one all along the line as to the distribution of patronage. Tomorrow it will be the Texas Wilson Democrats; the next day the Progressive Democrats of Alabama; then those of Maryland, of Kentucky, etc., who are urging that only those who have proven their sympathy with the administration be put on guard. And their adversaries will be there, too, ready to empurple Mr. Tumulty's carpet with sanguinary gore.

Mr. Montague, who was Governor of Virginia once, now has become a Congressman and might easily have been chosen for the Cabinet, but his errand this time is political and it is next to impossible to get to Mr. Wilson direct with a purely political appeal. At the outset of his administration President Wilson announced, to the consternation of the pie-hunters, that he himself would not receive candidates for office or their friends. Such as came to him he referred to the heads of the several departments. He went so far as to decline to talk with Congressmen and even Senators on the subject of patronage, and, though it has proven impossible to banish all discussion of candidates from the White House, the President has shown the utmost determination to save his energies just as far as possible for the real tasks of government, leaving the filling of offices to the members of his Cabinet. Nevertheless, during the early days of his term, candidates and their friends flocked to the executive offices. They came back the second day and the third day, the spark of hope still smoldering in their breasts. They stood about the secretary's office watching the slow hands of the clock that mark the hours eventful of so much in the nation's contemporaneous history and yet disappointing to so many personal ambitions.

Four of them who had been standing in a corner for hours one day caught the eye of an old statesman as he came out from his talk with the President; he turned and whispered to Mr. Tumulty: "They also *want to* serve who only stand and wait."

Here is a young man who spent last summer at the national headquarters; he had his salary, to be sure, but he thinks he ought to have "recognition" besides. The gray-bearded man sitting there is Mr. Henry Gassaway Davis—once the Democratic nominee for Vice-President of the United States. It is his second day on the scene; he was once a Senator, but he forgot yesterday that a cabinet day is scarcely one upon which a casual visitor can hope for a glimpse of the President. Mr. Marshall* has been in and has gone; wise man that he is, he was bent on no other errand than to pay a moment's respects to his chief, and he was satisfied to do that through the secretary.

Briskly moving about in animated conversation is a young man generally counted one of the new President's favorites—a pleasing enough chap with the weight of the world on his shoulders and the confidence in his ability to carry it in his eye. He has not yet given up hope of landing a $12,000 job with the aid of a father-in-law in the Senate. But he will not get in today.

Mr. Perry Belmont has come in to tell the President, if permitted to, that he made two speeches last night, one in Washington, the other in Baltimore, where he expatiated upon the signifi-

* Vice-President Thomas R. Marshall of Indiana [ed.].

cance of the New Freedom. Mayor Preston, of Baltimore, whose lavish (but unprofitable) hospitality delegates to the last Democratic convention will well remember, is here to invite the President to attend a performance to be given for the benefit of the families of men killed in the dynamite explosion at Baltimore. Over there, talking with Senator Luke Lea, is Representative Sims, of Tennessee; Mr. Sims had an appointment at this hour yesterday but was a minute and a half late and missed his chance.

Mr. Underwood, chairman of the Committee on Ways and Means, comes in on the dot for his appointment of half an hour. Mr. Underwood tells the President that his committee will have a tariff bill ready to report to Congress at the extra session to begin April 7.

The Secretary of War has twenty minutes' conference with the President, the two discussing the future of the Philippines.

A man enters, has a moment's whispered conversation with Mr. Tumulty, who takes him to the President irrespective of what is going on in the inner room. It is regarding the case of a soldier under sentence to die tomorrow in Arizona. A reprieve has suddenly become advisable; in two minutes the reprieve is granted.

The President is ahead of his schedule; there are three or four minutes to spare before the next visitor is due, and Mr. Wilson steps into the anteroom and greets the few callers gathered there. He steps briskly; always alert and vigorous, Mr. Wilson's movements have taken on a new vivacity, a new swiftness, since he came down to Washington. He was always a fast walker, for instance, but when he is seen on the streets here he is almost racing along. He moves about the executive offices with as rapid a pace as Roosevelt ever used, and he covers the distance between his office and the White House in breathless time. The fact is the President lives in constant dread of the office-seeker, who lies in wait at every door, in every passageway, along every path by which he hopes the President may pass.

There is a general hush as the President enters the secretary's room. Everybody is instantly on his feet. Very rapidly Mr. Wilson passes from man to man, usually with nothing more than a smile of greeting and a handshake; here and there, a low petition is spoken; now and again a paper comes out of a pocket. It is all over in a moment, however, and the dark designs of a dozen aspirants have been frustrated. They have "paid their respects," the errand on which they ostensibly came, and they have not preferred the requests which they expected casually to mention. When Theodore Roosevelt used to come prancing out into the waiting room, the air was suddenly filled with the sputter and crackle of words discharged like rifle shots. When Taft came out, the room was ' suddenly one broad smile. He made the rounds, pretended to listen, cracked a little joke here and there, and disappeared in a general gasp of merriment. Woodrow Wilson can laugh as heartily as anyone, but when about this business of the Presidency he doesn't; the benignancy of his nature shines through a face usually serious and very often overcast with deepest gravity.

Very swiftly, the room fills up again. In comes Senator Ransdell, of Louisiana, and Colonel Robert Ewing of that state. The sugar schedule requires much looking after. The editor of an Atlanta newspaper is on time for his appointment. This newcomer, pulling at a piratical moustache greatly at odds with his cherubic face, is Delaware's new Senator, Willard Saulsbury.

But now approaches the sensation of the morning, in the person of William Jennings Bryan. He has just passed through the salvos of the camera batteries at the entrance, his celebrated grin outdoing the best performance of the Cheshire cat; Mr. Bryan seems a very happy man and is winning new friends every minute, moving, as he does, surrounded by a magnetic field. It is five minutes before the President learns of his chief minister's arrival; then the two go into the little room for a half hour of intimate talk.

Mr. McAdoo has a way of slipping in by the other entrance. Today he brings with him George Foster Peabody—one man who, in spite of his reputed Democracy, is trying to keep out of office.

News has just been handed in from the telegraph room that the New Hampshire legislature deadlock is broken, and Hollis, the Democrat, is elected United States Senator. "Good!" cries the President, for a moment forgetting some serious business in hand, and "Good!" echo twenty lusty throats.

Just as the Gridiron Club delegation comes in—six of the best-looking, at all events of the best-fed, members of that famous association of writers and fun-makers. They have come armed to the teeth with six unanswerable speeches. Unanswerable and un-answered—because never made. The President capitulated on sight. He will appear at the next Gridiron dinner. The interview, scheduled for ten minutes, lasted fifty seconds.

The wife of a Princeton professor has waited till half past one to exchange a word with Mr. Wilson. The opportunity comes at last.

So the procession comes, pauses, and passes. You wonder what possible impression its members can hope to make upon the wearied retina, the tired tympanum, of the man in the Oval Room.

The case is not what one would expect. The President's mind and nerves have much the quality of youth. They are singularly fresh and tenacious; they function like a boy's both in receiving and recording impressions. He hears and sees and does not easily forget. Let us go into the Oval Room.

It is a cabinet, perhaps 25 by 35 feet, done in light olive-green burlap with white wainscoting and doors. At one end is a fireplace with a white marble mantel, on it a French clock under a glass dome; opposite, a deep bay window. Glazed bookcases are set into the wainscoting between the doors; the floor is covered with a plain green rug of domestic manufacture. A solitary picture still hangs—or did hang, the other day—as if forgotten, on one wall: a small photograph of Theodore Roosevelt. The President sits at his desk in the bay of the window; another chair is placed at one end of the desk. At one side of this main chamber there is a smaller room in dark brown, furnished with a couch and easy chairs, and a tiny desk set into the wall; to this room on rare occasions the President may retire with a particularly favored visitor. Beyond this is the cabinet room, a rectangular chamber none too large for its big table with ten chairs somewhat crowded around it; there is no place provided for the seat of the Secretary of Labor, and he sits doubled up with the Secretary of Commerce at the lower end. The cabinet room is done in light brown; maps and law books line the walls, and a globe stands in the middle of the floor. The only picture is a Lincoln over the mantel. For a change of scene the President sometimes leads his visitors into the cabinet room.

An interview with Mr. Wilson is always a delightful and satisfactory affair. Not always, of course, in its results, for the United States now has a President who can say "no" as easily as "yes," though he knows how to take the sting out of a refusal, if he wants to. But an interview is always delightful and satisfactory in that the visitor has the fullest opportunity to tell his story and make his request or his argument, assured of an attentive hearing. All visitors agree that Mr. Wilson has a peculiar faculty of putting them at their best; not a few timid, unready talkers have told me wonderingly that in his company they found their tongues unloosed and their ideas flowing rapidly into appropriate words. Appraised as austere by the public which does not know him, Mr. Wilson is in fact a man of ready and profound sympathy. All feel that instantly on coming into contact with him. He has no tricks of manner; he is innocent of any design to appear cordial; but the genuine simplicity of his look and of his words is inevitably winning. He is a shy man himself, if the truth were known, and perhaps it is the most timid of men who are the best understood by him.

Mr. Wilson is the best listener that has been in the White House for many a year. Mr. Roosevelt never listened to anybody in his life, of course; Mr. Taft could listen well, when interested, but people often suspected that Mr. Taft's mind was awandering, even while his face was attentive. You never have that feeling with Mr. Wilson. It is apparent from the first word that he is closely following you; as a rule he is silent until you have concluded; sometimes, however, his face will light up and he will nod or let a soft "yes" pass his lips. You have the feeling that his mind is ahead of you, as in fact it is, and you pass rapidly from point to point, well satisfied with your own swift eloquence. Then, instantly, you get your reply, and it is perfectly clear that Mr. Wilson has taken you all in—all you have said, some things you have left unsaid. His mind leaps to respond.

All Washington agrees that it is a simple delight to have converse with the new President. I have seen his swiftness of apprehension and his clean-cut clearness of mind displayed on hundreds of occasions in Princeton and Trenton, and it was no surprise to me to hear visitors emerge from interviews at the White House with their faces glowing with the pleasure of having transacted their business so satisfactorily; no surprise to hear Secretaries praise, as if it were something unheard of and impossible in political life, the directness, swiftness, accuracy, and precision of the operations of the mind under whose Presidency they sit around the cabinet table.

"There was not an irrelevant word," said one visitor, coming away; "he listened like a judge, and answered instantly, speaking precisely to the subject I had raised, and not to some other subject."

More than one visitor has noticed, however, that after he has ventured warily to approach the question of patronage the President's responsiveness has suddenly flagged and, without any direct refusal to listen to a statement of the claims of the candidate, the change that has fallen over the spirit of the meeting has effectually prevented its utterance.

"I simply cannot understand," Mr. Wilson has said in my hearing, "the passion that goes into this struggle for office; I cannot understand the deep personal feeling with which the advocates of this man or that argue in season and out of season for their candidate, or the resentment with which they hear a rival mentioned.

"Of course, if I were to allow myself to listen to all this turmoil of importunate candidacies I could do nothing else. There would be nothing but the ragged shreds of a mind to give to the real business of the nation, with which I am charged."

Yet Mr. Wilson is a man whose sympathies are so readily engaged that it is likely many a case will get past his guard, to worry and encumber him. Some of the candidates and friends of candidates who presume on that sympathy, though, will be wiser when they have made their attempt. Mr. Wilson is a gentleman and a scholar, but he is—I speak whereof I do know and testify what I have seen—capable of giving the thickest-skinned politician a colorful quarter of an hour.

In subtler ways, too, he is disconcerting, when he wants to be. The deliberation with which he adjusts his nose-glasses and studies a visitor is sometimes suggestive, and the long gold pencil and the neat little memorandum book—with and in which, having carefully produced them, sometimes he maliciously sets about making very precise entries—are likely to become famous engines of destruction, as the country learns about the conversations that take place in the ivory and white room.

His capacity for sustained gravity, too, is a magnificent weapon.

A committee of suffragists visited him the other day, and the ladies were not unimpressed with the seriousness of their mission. When they came out, the chairman said:

"It was the most solemn meeting I ever attended. The President was cordial, but grave. We took in a copy of Mr. Wilson's book, *The New Freedom,* and told him that by substituting 'women' for 'men' in some paragraphs it would make the best argument for woman's suffrage ever written. At that a fleeting smile stole over the Presidential visage. Then we all relapsed into solemnity. We said our pieces and we were as solemn as owls. But an owl would seem as merry as a lark by the side of the President. Where we made a mistake was in not bringing in a coffin and turning it into a funeral."

President Wilson enjoyed that interview as much as the ladies did.

The majority of the President's callers already come to discuss policies. As soon as the first stream of purely congratulatory calls had ceased, Mr. Wilson began the discussion with visitors of the great public problems of the nation. There was a day or two when his callers seemed to think that, like his predecessors, he must be occupying himself at the beginning of his term with appointments. They found it was not so, as I have said; that already the question of patronage had been relegated to a place in the back of his mind; that he was eager to advance to serious discussions of principles. Already, before he had been in the White House a week, he was deep in the question of the attitude to be taken toward Mexico and Central America; of the proper relations of the government to the Chinese republic and to the policy of the "dollar diplomacy"; of the tariff, and the extremely practical problems of the preparation of a bill that would pass both Houses of Congress; of the currency, the establishment of a great fiscal system of a new breadth and stability. Already, also, President Wilson was taking up details of the government, and some of its specific problems. Within two weeks of his inauguration, he had announced the position of his administration with regard to the two chief concerns of our foreign policy: our attitude toward Latin America and toward China. The atmosphere about the White House from the start filled every visitor with the feeling that not a moment was to be lost; four years was not a day too long in which to do the great things for which the people have commissioned this administration.

Things pass very rapidly in the Oval Room. A "yes," a memorandum on a pad, a touch of the bell summoning a clerk, a dozen times an hour starts the making of a bit of history. Occasionally, a secretary or a confidential stenographer comes in softly and lays before the President a paper to which a red tag is clipped—an "important and urgent" signal. All through the rest of the building the air is palpitant with excitement. The newspapermen at the door scrutinize eagerly every entrance and departure, slip in and out of Mr. Tumulty's office to "get a line on" one or another of a dozen mysterious rumors always current; the official staff, long habituated to rapid and important events, is keyed to the highest pitch in its effort to regard and execute the decisions of the man at the center of all this activity. But there is no excitement there, no haste. If ever a man was born to govern, Mr. Wilson was; to govern confidently, though graciously. Here he is, this student of thirty cloistered years who had never been inside the White House until the day of his inauguration, to whom the city of Washington was still practically unknown—here he is, sitting in the very center of the nation's business and setting about the administration of its government with the grave but easy confidence, the poise and equanimity, of one born to the heritage of the chief chair of state, trained from his childhood in its expected duties, and experienced for years in their execution. There is no assumption of knowing everything; very often indeed there is a naïve confession of ignorance and a request for information from the visitor. But with the utmost simplicity, there is also always an absolute and almost innocent faith in the power of a pure heart and a single eye.

The President's mornings (his mornings last until half past one) are too fully occupied by appointments to allow of his holding the public receptions in which his predecessors used to indulge at the noon hour. The custom has arisen, as I have said, of giving visitors without appointments cards admitting them to the East Room of the White House at half past two in the afternoon.

The East Room, running the depth of the mansion, with windows on three sides, with its four great fireplaces, three crystal chandeliers, its mirrors, its ornate decorations of white and gold, is very different from the rather shabby, businesslike quarters in which the work of the morning is done. Under the direction of doorkeepers, visitors are lined up around the walls—for several hundred callers seek to greet the President at these levees. Promptly at two thirty the great door swings open and, preceded by a smart aide in military uniform, the President steps rapidly out and takes a position in the center of the floor. The President has donned a black frock coat now, and the scene is more formal.

The procession past him begins. Each person, introduced by the aide, shakes the President's hand and presents his greetings or performs his errand. At the head of the line one day is Colonel Eustis, chairman of the Inauguration Committee, supported by a few of his colleagues, who have come to present Mr. Wilson with the medal cast to commemorate the inauguration. Three Commissioners of the District of Columbia present their compliments. Next in line is a character who calls himself the "King of the Newsboys." The "King" says a formal little speech and gets a word of good will for the juvenile disseminators of diurnal literature. Mr. Samuel Untermyer is in line; as is the retiring Solicitor General—Mr. Bullitt has a good deal of manners and makes his little speech of good-by as happily as if it were one of gratitude.

A little further down the line is someone bearing a large photograph which he begs the President to accept. Others have photographs which they beg to have autographed. Here is a Congressman introducing a mother of an army officer who has fallen into difficulty. Here is a Senator with two of his important constituents who have a request to prefer. Next comes a lady, an old acquaintance, who brings her little daughter for the grace of a greeting from the President.

Perhaps one third of those in line have some particular word to say or request to make; the majority, however, have come merely to wish the President luck. And it is very evident in most cases that the wish is sincere and even profound. It is a very instructive and touching thing to watch for a few days this procession at the afternoon receptions, and to observe the attitude toward their President of the representatives of the mass of the people with nothing to ask. They come from all parts of the country: "Tennessee," "Indiana," "Kansas," "Rhode Island," succeeding one another as the introductions are made. They show no great originality in their way of expressing their feelings; commonly they utter one of the commonplace salutations of ordinary life; they wish him "luck" in one phrase or another. But whether it be that for the average citizen his presentation to the President is a rare moment, or whether it be that Woodrow Wilson has already gained an unusual place in the affections of the people, it is impossible not to see that the good wishes have an intensity of feeling behind them. I was surprised and impressed to remark how many different sorts of people—prosperous-looking men, benevolent-looking old ladies, brisk young chaps—said: "God bless you!" So spoke scores. I think the President must have been touched by this exercise of the priestly function of a people by the spontaneous lips of its representatives. I fancy he must find no little inspiration in this daily benediction. "Up from the common soil, up from the quiet heart of the people, rise the streams of hope and eulogy," he has said again and again.

✪

Wilson on Himself

I was just thinking of my sense of confusion of identity, some-times, when I read the articles about myself. I have never read an article about myself in which I have recognized myself, and I have come to have the impression that I must be some kind of a fraud, because I think a great many of these articles are written in absolute good faith. I tremble to think of the variety and falseness in the impressions I make—and it is being borne in on me so that it may change my very disposition—that I am a cold and removed person who has a thinking machine inside which he adjusts to the circumstances, which he does not allow to be moved by any winds of affection or emotion of any kind, that turns like a cold search-light on anything that is presented to his attention and makes it work.

I am not aware of having any detachable apparatus inside of me. On the contrary, if I were to interpret myself, I would say that my constant embarrassment is to restrain the emotions that are inside of me. You may not believe it, but I sometimes feel like a fire from a far from extinct volcano, and if the lava does not seem to spill over it is because you are not high enough to see the

A speech to the National Press Club, Washington, March 20, 1914, re-printed from Ray Stannard Baker and William E. Dodd (eds.), *The Public Papers of Woodrow Wilson: The New Democracy* (2 vols., New York: Harper & Brothers, 1926), pp. 94–98.

caldron boil. Because, truly, gentlemen, in the position which I now occupy there is a sort of, I do not know how else to express it than to say, passionate sense of being connected with my fellow-men in a peculiar relationship of responsibility, not merely the responsibility of office, but God knows there are enough things in this world that need to be corrected.

I have mixed, first and last, with all sorts and conditions of men—there are mighty few kinds of men that have to be described to me, and there are mighty few kinds of experiences that have to be described to me—and when I think of the number of men who are looking to me as the representative of a party, with the hope for all varieties of salvage from the things they are struggling in the midst of, it makes me tremble. It makes me tremble not only with a sense of my own inadequacy and weakness, but as if I were shaken by the very things that are shaking them and, if I seem circumspect, it is because I am so diligently trying not to make any colossal blunders. If you just calculate the number of blunders a fellow can make in twenty-four hours if he is not careful and if he does not listen more than he talks, you would see something of the feeling that I have.

I was amused the other day at a remark that Senator Newlands made. I had read him the trust message that I was to deliver to Congress some ten days before I delivered it, and I never stop "doctoring" things of that kind until the day I have to deliver them. When he heard it read to Congress he said: "I think it was better than it was when you read it to me." I said: "Senator, there is one thing which I do not think you understand. I not only use all the brains I have, but all I can borrow, and I have borrowed a lot since I read it to you first."

That, I dare say, is what gives the impression of circumspect-ness. I am listening; I am diligently trying to collect all the brains that are borrowable in order that I will not make more blunders than it is inevitable that a man should make who has great limitations of knowledge and capacity. And the emotion of the thing is so great that I suppose I must be some kind of a mask to conceal it. I really feel sometimes as if I were masquerading when I catch a picture of myself in some printed description. In between things that I have to do as a public officer I never think of myself as the President of the United States, because I never have had any sense of being identified with that office.

I feel like a person appointed for a certain length of time to administer that office, and I feel just as much outside of it at this moment as I did before I was elected to it. I feel just as much outside of it as I still feel outside of the government of the United States. No man could imagine himself the government of the United States; but he could understand that some part of his fellow citizens had told him to go and run a certain part of it the best he knew how. That would not make him the government itself or the thing itself. It would just make him responsible for running it the best he knew how. The machine is so much greater than himself, the office is so much greater than he can ever be, and the most he can do is to look grave enough and self-possessed enough to seem to fill it.

I can hardly refrain every now and again from tipping the public the wink, as much as to say, "It is only 'me' that is inside this thing. I know perfectly well that I will have to get out presently. I know that then I will look just my own proper size, and that for the time being the proportions are somewhat refracted and misrepresented to the eye by the large thing I am inside of, from which I am tipping you this wink."

For example, take matters of this sort. I will not say whether it is wise or unwise, simple or grave, but certain precedents have been established that in certain companies the President must leave the room first, and people must give way to him. They must not sit down if he is standing up. It is a very uncomfortable thing to have to think of all the other people every time I get up and sit down, and all that sort of thing. So that when I get guests in my own house and the public is shut out I adjourn being President and take leave to be a gentleman. If they draw back and insist upon my doing something first, I firmly decline.

There are blessed intervals when I forget by one means or another that I am President of the United States. One means by which I forget is to get a rattling good detective story, get after some imaginary offender, and chase him all over—preferably any continent but this, because the various parts of this continent are becoming painfully suggestive to me. The post offices, and many other things which stir reminiscence have "sicklied them o'er with a pale cast of thought." There are post offices to which I wouldn't think of mailing a letter, which I can't think of without trembling with the knowledge of all the heartburnings of the struggle there was in getting somebody installed as postmaster.

Now, if I were free I would come not infrequently up to these rooms. You know I never was in Washington but for a very few times, and for a very few hours, until I came last year, and I never expect to see the inside of the public buildings in Washington until my term is over. The minute I turn up anywhere I am personally conducted to beat the band. The curator and the assistant curator and every other blooming official turns up, and they show me so much attention that I don't see the building. I would have to say "Stand aside and let me see what you are showing me."

Some day after I am through with this office I am going to come back to Washington and see it. In the meantime I am in the same category as the National Museum, the Monument, the Smithsonian Institution, or the Congressional Library, and everything that comes down here has to be shown the President. If I only knew the appearance to assume—apparently I can assume other appearances that do not show what is going on inside—I would like to have it pointed out, so that I could practice it before the looking glass and see if I could not look like the Monument. Being regarded as a national exhibit, it will be much simpler than being shaken hands with by the whole United States.

And yet, even that is interesting to me, simply because I like

human beings. It is a pretty poor crowd that does not interest you.
I think they would have to be all members of that class that
devotes itself to "expense regardless of pleasure" in order to be
entirely uninteresting. These look so much alike—spend their time
trying to look so much alike—and so relieve themselves of all
responsibility of thought that they are very monotonous, indeed, to
look at; whereas, a crowd picked up off the street is just a jolly
lot—a job lot of real human beings, pulsating with life, with all
kinds of passions and desires.

It would be a great pleasure if, unobserved and unattended, I
could be knocked around as I have been accustomed to being
knocked around all my life; if I could resort to any delightful
quarter, to any place in Washington that I chose. I have sometimes
thought of going to some costumer's—some theatrical costumer's
—and buying an assortment of beards, rouge and coloring and all
the known means of disguising myself, if it were not against the
law.

You see I have a scruple as President against breaking the law
and disguising one's self is against the law, but if I could disguise
myself and not get caught I would go out, be a free American
citizen once more and have a jolly time. I might then meet some of
you gentlemen and actually tell you what I really thought.

✪

Reflections on the Presidency

We were sitting in his private study on the second floor of the White House at eight of an evening in early December. He had just completed his address to Congress and had sent it to the printer; and his desk was still littered with scraps of paper on which there were notes in his minute handwriting, with books and documents and all the paraphernalia for address-making.

The President had taken the chair he uses for his work at the desk. He had pulled it round and had asked me to take a seat nearby. He slid easily into a most comfortable attitude, with one hand in a trousers pocket and the elbow of his other arm resting on the arm of the chair. He leaned back in the chair, crossed his legs, made a sort of circle of the thumb and first finger of the hand not pocketed, and peered at me through the circle. There was a twinkle in his eye.

"Now," he said, "what shall we talk about?"

"Well," I suggested tentatively, "the world is full of a number of things."

"It is," he replied; "but a good many of them are not talkable subjects at the present time."

From Samuel G. Blythe, "A Talk with the President," *Saturday Evening Post,* CLXXXVII (January 9, 1915), pp. 3-4, 37-38. Reprinted with permission from *The Saturday Evening Post.* Copyright 1915 by The Curtis Publishing Company.

So we took preparedness for war, and business, and currency, and trusts, and Mexico, and the shipping problem, and rural credits, and the European war—especially the European war— and set them up on the mantelpiece—squat, grouchy little mani- kins of pressing problems that had been and are pressing—and left them, in a scowling, uneasy row, to jostle one another and growl over the lack of appreciation of their importance, and went gayly to our talk, regardless of the mutterings of the grouchy pressing- problem manikins and their efforts to edge themselves into the conversation.

That was last night. And this morning, as I am writing, I have taken some more things and put them alongside the others. I have set up there what was said about the philosophy and psychology of politics; of the vitality and adaptability of the Constitition; of motives of various persons; of the maneuvering of various intri- gants; of numerous abstract considerations and corollaries— because I want to write a human document about one of the most human men I ever met or knew.

There is a general disposition to regard the President as a think- ing machine, as a large and brilliant but gelid intellect, encased in a nonresponsive and highly insulated covering. He is thought of and talked of as mostly brains—and cold, analytical, logical brains at that; and there can be no denying that he has those commodities in full supply. The other side of him is not so generally known, principally because his rise in public life has been so rapid and his transfer from academy to arena occurred so few years ago.

Wherefore, it seems about the proper time to set down the fact here that Woodrow Wilson, President of the United States, is one of the most kindly, courteous, considerate, genial and companion- able of men; that, so far from being aloof from the people, his passion is the people—the real people—and his sole desire is to serve them so long as his term of office shall continue, and after- ward in such measure as he may. He holds his position to be that of a man connected with his fellow-men by a peculiar relationship of responsibility, and the vivid sense of that responsibility is doubtless accountable for the impression of aloofness. However, that is not what I started out to say. The point that presses at this time is that the President of the United States weighs one hundred and seventy-six pounds, and that those one hundred and seventy-six pounds are mostly bone and muscle. There is not an ounce of excess baggage in the way of flesh about him. He lives out-of-doors as much as he can. His face is tanned and so are his sinewy hands. His eye is bright and clear. His laugh is hearty and unaffected. His spirit is good. He is buoyantly healthy. He sleeps well, eats well, works hard, and plays whenever he has a chance.

His principal recreation is golf. He plays every day, usually with Dr. Grayson, and goes to most of the links about Washington. . . .

I talked with him intimately for more than two hours, and there was not a syllable from him about the great war; not an intimation that he knew there was a war; not an opinion or a comment, though he has forty war problems before him every day.

And, of course, the talk came to politics. I said that, in my opinion, and from my experience, the actuating motives in politics are vanity and jealousy.

"Yes," the President replied; "that is true—or egotism, rather, which amounts to the same thing. My father was a Presbyterian minister and all that implies in the very highest sense. On Sunday afternoons, after his sermon in the morning, he used to lie down on the couch by the fire. I would sit on the rug beside him and we would have wonderful talks. He told me once, I remember, when discussing this subject, that the old casuists had resolved all sins into the one great sin of egotism, because that consists in putting oneself before God."

He made a wry face.

"I don't suppose," he said, "that any man has greater opportunity than I to discover that the predominant trait in humans and in politics is vanity—egotism—the exaltation of self. This recalls a visit I had recently from a most able man, a man I have known for years, who is genuinely talented, highly cultured, affable and conscientious, and honest and correct in his usual relations with men. Still, when anything comes that bears any relation to himself —to his exalted ego—he forgets every principle he has, and fore- stalls all his culture and all his kindness to get for himself what he deems he deserves, because of his intense egotism.

"I found this out long before I went into public life. I discovered it soon after I became the head of Princeton, and it has been impressed on me more and more in my service as Governor of New Jersey and in my service here. The truly great politician—the statesman—you know, is the man who can take an impersonal view of politics—the impersonal view."

"But," I interrupted, "you do not find many of that kind, do you?"

"I think," the President replied, "that every really great man in politics, either in this country or abroad, was impersonal in his relations to his politics and his place. Take Lincoln, for example. You remember the stories of his troubles with Stanton, his Secre- tary of War? One of them is that once, when Lincoln sent an order to Stanton, Stanton tore up the order, refused to obey it, and said to the messenger:

" 'You go back and tell Lincoln he is a damned fool!'

"The man went back and told Mr. Lincoln.

" 'Did Stanton say I am a damned fool?' the President asked.

" 'He did.'

" 'Well,' said Lincoln, 'Stanton generally knows what he is talking about.'

"That's what I mean," continued the President earnestly—"the power to subtract one's personality from the subject at hand. It is more necessary here than elsewhere. One cannot consider these problems as an individual. One must consider them impersonally, as an executive, appointed for a certain time to administer the office he holds, with due regard to the requirements of the people, and not in any sense with regard to his own predilections or prejudices or passions. I am responsible for running the government as best I know how; but I am not the government. The people are the government."

"I heard Premier Asquith say practically the same thing," I said.

"Yes," continued the President; "but we have the better of Asquith in a way. Asquith is more vitally the government of England, with his Cabinet, than we are the government over here, for Asquith and his ministers sit in the Commons; they are there to be questioned, and to direct, and to demand support, and to meet opposition. If they are defeated they can go directly to the country for support or rejection. They have to take part. Whereas, over here, if the Congress requires anything of a member of the Cabinet, say, and he does not see fit to answer that requirement, he can say an answer is not compatible with the public welfare, and let it go at that. We have greater power and less direct responsibility."

"Well, Mr. President," I said, "you are on the inside in this place, looking out, and the rest of the world is on the outside, looking in. What is the most interesting thing about the Presidency from your viewpoint?"

"The power of decision," he replied. "The knowledge that I, by virtue of the position I hold, can decide matters that are of moment to our people and to the rest of the world. With that, of course, comes the tremendous sense of responsibility; but that is the most interesting thing—painfully interesting at times, painfully!

"And," he went on animatedly, "I discover that I am not relying entirely on any present situation when I am called on to make these important decisions. By that I mean the influence which directs me isn't entirely the present influence—the influence exerted by the particular set of circumstances at hand—but is a culminative influence predicated on information I have secured in former times, of former circumstances, and of former procedure.

"That is to say, I have stored away in my mind, to be drawn on, a certain amount of information that comes to be of the greatest use in such contingencies. When a phase of a question comes up before me I not only consider that phase or that question in view of the present circumstances but in view of past circumstances. I suppose I am helped in this because I once wrote a history of the United States.

"Let me tell you why I wrote that history. I had no particular intention of being a historian. That was not in my mind. What was in my mind was to write a book on the development and philosophy of American politics. I wanted to do that. But when I came to do it I soon found I did not know enough to write such a book. I had not the information. So, in order to learn the history I needed, I wrote a history. Some time before I wrote that history I had written an essay telling how history should be written.

"When I wrote that essay I had no idea I should become a historian; and when I wrote my history I discovered that my performance did not measure up at all to the critical requirements I had laid down in the essay I had written, discussing the proper manner in which history should be written. My mistake was in laying down rules before I began the practice. Probably if I should write such an essay now, it would conform more closely to my performance than to my propaganda.

"Then I came into public life; and the book about politics is yet to be written."

"But you will write it," I said.

"Yes; I shall write it," he answered—"provided there is anything left of me when I get through with this job."

"The thing that has most impressed me about the Presidency since I began to know about Presidents is the incredible loneliness of the man in it," I said.

"Yes," the President replied; "it is a lonely place. It is necessarily solitary. Human nature is so constituted that a position of advantage invariably is utilized by the person occupying it. A

President can have no intimates; because, no matter how unselfish those intimates may be at the beginning, inevitably they will seek to take advantage of that intimacy before the end. A President has so much to give, you know; and good resolutions of unselfish behavior cannot withstand the pressure of the temptation to ask for something on an opportunity provided by that intimacy.

"It is a lonely place; but that very loneliness has its compensations, and those compensations are great. Standing alone here I feel and know that I am in closer conscious touch with the people. I can hear them better; sense their wants and their dues better; come closer to them than I could if I were surrounded by a group, either large or small, who were constantly dinning into my ears their own thoughts, ideas, desires and opinions. I am in closer conscious touch with the outside. There are no walls of selfish humans between me and the country. There is no babble of nearby voices to deafen my ears to the real demands from the great outside."

The President rose, walked to the window, and motioned for me to come and stand beside him. He pulled back the curtain and pointed out over the great sweep of the White House lawn, where the spray of the fountain glittered in the moonlight; where the shadows of the naked trees were sharply silhouetted on the turf; where, beyond, the Monument stood silvery in the light; and where the dome of the Capitol rose majestically in the far distance.

"Often," he said, "I stand here and look out over this picture; and I say to myself: 'This isn't Washington, with its petty politics and its little strifes, and its concentration of interests, and its puny ambitions and jealousies and egotisms and vanities and intrigues. This is the wide country—the busy East; the sweep of the prairies of the West; the breath of the forests; the grandeur of the mountains.' I am not shut up here. I am in conscious relation with all the people; and that, my dear friend, is the compensating advantage for the loneliness of my place.

"I love my fellow-man. No person takes keener delight in his society than I do. I have my friends and I love them; but I realize that the circumscriptions of my position are not an unmixed evil. I may be lonely because of the necessities of my place; but my vision is clearer than it would be were I surrounded by a group—any group—of well-meaning and zealous friends with interests of their own.

"Do not misunderstand me, I beg of you. Do not think or say that I take no delight in the society of my fellows. No man is more gregarious than I. As Lincoln said: 'I reckon no man likes his fellow-men better than I do—and no man sees less of them socially.' It goes with the place, and, as I have explained, it is not altogether undesirable."

We stood there for a minute silently. Then he put his hand on my shoulder and we walked back to our chairs.

"What," I asked, "is the most disagreeable feature of the Presidency?"

"Patronage," he replied without a moment's hesitation— "patronage, and the genuine astonishment and resentment of personal friends that I cannot take care of them merely because they are personal friends. Politics, you know, as it is widely considered, consists in taking care of one's personal friends. Now I should like to do that, love to do it; but I cannot. And I am constantly perplexed at the genuine aggrievement of those friends because I cannot and do not.

"I would willingly take the coat off my back and give it to a friend who needed it. My friends can have anything I have that is mine; but I cannot give them what is not mine. These offices are not mine. They belong to the people. They are the nation's. Merely because a man is a personal friend of mine, or has been something or other that makes him think he is, is not a valid reason for bestowing on him an office that does not belong to me, but is mine only to administer through the proper person selected as the active agent. The obligation incumbent on me, as the distributor for the moment of these offices, is to find efficient men to hold them, not personal friends to hold them and get the emoluments.

"I do not think my generosity or my sense of deep and lasting friendship for my real friends can be questioned; but there is a higher obligation than any personal obligation: that is my obligation to the people of this country, who have put me in this place temporarily to administer their governmental affairs for them and who demand of me that I shall administer them for the people and not for the individual, even though that individual be myself or someone close to me.

"Moreover," he went on, his voice vibrant with earnestness and sincerity, "it is my firm impression that patronage ruins more potentially great men than any other one political influence. By that I mean that many a man who comes into public life hampers his true development by his devotion to patronage hunting, and his limitations thereby, more than in any other way. They spend their time running to get a job here and a job there.

"Of course there is a reason for it, because most of them owe their positions in public life to the work of the men back home, and they feel they must do what can be done for those men, and for their own men—the organization—in order that they may have future and continued success at the polls. But, as my observation goes, many a man in public life has not developed to half of his true capacity because of this ceaseless devotion to the harassing details of patronage. Some of them, to be sure, wouldn't develop very much if there were no patronage; but it is my firm opinion that if patronage could be eliminated we should have a bigger, broader, more patriotic and more useful body of legislators than we now have.

"I am not insensible to the demands made on public men who, in their turn, make those demands on me; but I deprecate them. I see fierce contests over federal offices; consume hour after hour listening to the claims of one set of men or another; and I am convinced that, except for mere organization purposes, the people, as a mass, are not interested and do not pretend to be.

"Take the postmastership of any of our large cities, for example. When one of those contests for appointment is on, you would think, to hear the proponents and opponents of the candidates tell it, that the very foundations of the republic will rock if one man is not appointed or if another man is. And yet, I venture to say, the only concern of the great mass of the people over the postmastership of one city is that they get their mail promptly and that the office is administered honestly and efficiently. Let me repeat: If patronage could be eliminated we should have a much broader, more patriotic, more capable and more useful set of legislators."

"Is patronage the chief of your troubles?" I asked.

The President turned and looked at me with a sort of quizzical smile on his face.

"Troubles!" he exclaimed. "Troubles! Why, my dear sir, the White House is the clearing house for trouble!"

He stopped and laughed—laughed with his head thrown back and his shoulders shaking.

"After I was elected," he said, "and before I came to Washington, many advisers sought me to advise. Most of them told me, with solemn portent, that the thing I must guard against most was flattery.

" 'Beware,' they exhorted, 'of the fawning sycophant! Steel yourself against the insidious flatterer. Do not be misled by the words of the honeyed tongue.' "

He laughed again.

"It's a joke," he said—"a joke. I haven't been bothered with flatterers. Of course there are some few obvious glad-handers who can be set down instantly where they belong; but, you may believe me, there has been no excess of flattery since I have been here. No person comes to you when things are going right. That is expected. Every person comes to you when things are going wrong. That is what I meet with day after day—trouble, complaint, things that have gone wrong, things that have bogged down. They want me to straighten them out. They want help. They want to tell me their troubles—and they do; you may be quite sure they do.

"The White House is the clearing house for trouble—not only Washington troubles, departmental troubles, governmental troubles, but hundreds and hundreds of the people write here to tell their private grievances and to ask for redress or for my aid. When things are going right we hear little about them; but when things go wrong we hear all about them—and there is no flattery about it, either. Flattery hasn't bothered me in the least. I don't have to fend off flatterers. My defensive tactics are employed against kickers." . . .

We talked of many other things, discussing various statesmen and the correctness of certain policies. He showed me why a writer was wrong who said he could not be a progressive Democrat if he admired Edmund Burke, and explained his liking for Burke and quoted much from Burke's orations.

The President said he intends to make some speeches on his return from the San Francisco Exposition next spring—"because," he remarked, "I shall have something to say to the people then. I have felt that it was not for me to appear in the role of a prophet before the people; but when this Congress is over we shall have a substantial record of things achieved, and I want to talk to the people about what we have done—not about what we intend to do."

He commented on the recent elections,* expressing his satisfaction over the fact that, as he views it, the Democratic party is now a majority party and has great hopes for the future.

"I remember you said once that you read detective stories," I remarked. "Do you still read them?"

"I devour them," he replied. "I mean, of course, the better class of detective stories.

* The midterm elections of 1914 [ed.].

"I like the theater, too, and especially a good vaudeville show when I am seeking perfect relaxation; for a vaudeville show is different from a play, though I am intensely interested in the drama in all its phases. Still, if there is a bad act at a vaudeville show you can rest reasonably secure that the next one may not be so bad; but from a bad play there is no escape. Of course"—and he turned his face away—"I cannot go to the theater now."

He walked over to the window.

"Good night, Mr. President," I said.

"Good night, Blythe," he answered, and as I turned at the door he was still standing by the window, looking, with misty eyes, at the great Monument, towering silvery in the cold moonlight.

RAY STANNARD BAKER

✪

Wilson as President: An Appraisal

One fragrant summer night not long ago I walked through the unguarded outer gate up to the White House. It was at the height of one of the great moments in the present world crisis. Newsboys were calling a late extra on the streets: I could hear the curiously disquieting note they contrive, on such occasions, to impart to their voices, without catching the words they cried—was it Germany or Mexico, or some new peril? One had the sense of vast impending events.

But nothing, certainly, could be calmer, more soothing, that feverish night, than the aspect of the executive mansion and the quiet and shady grounds around it. There was a fragrance of flowers in the air and somewhere among the trees I could hear the night twitter of birds. I seemed to have stepped suddenly out of a tempestuous world into a garden of silence. Not a policeman, much less a soldier, was visible, no guards of any kind, and I walked up to the door as one would walk up to the home of a friend—wondering a little what a stranger from a war-torn European capital would have thought of this exhibition of unguarded power.

From Ray Stannard Baker, "Wilson," *Collier's,* LVIII (October 7, 1916), 5–6, 41. Copyright 1916 by *Collier's;* reprinted by permission of Rachel Baker Napier in behalf of the heirs of Ray Stannard Baker.

Inside there was the same utter quietude—two men at the door—and upstairs in his private study, a workroom with a typewriter in the corner, a business-looking filing cabinet, a desk piled high with documents and books, sat the President of the United States, quietly, steadily, patiently—and rather lonesomely—working at his enormous and critical task. A large painting on the wall took on, at the moment, some casual significance—it was that of McKinley and Day signing the treaty of peace with the Spanish ambassador after the Cuban war.

I think sometimes the flashing impression of such a moment more interpretive than anything actually seen or heard. It all came to me that night—the undisturbed home, the peaceful surroundings, the thoughtful man at his desk—curiously but deeply as a symbol of immense strength. Here at the center of things where the spirit of the nation questioned itself was a great quietude, steadiness, confidence. If the nation were really afraid, if it really distrusted itself or its leadership in this world crisis, there would be evidence of it, some increased palpitation, here at the heart of things. Our American Presidents, more than any statesmen in the world, I suppose, are true *public* men. There are few "state secrets," little concealment, much frankness. Mr. Roosevelt told everybody pretty nearly everything and put it all the next day in a letter or a speech. I recall seeing him not long after he was settled in the White House, and of coming away quite bowed down with the weight of high matters of state which had been imparted to me. Outside I met my friend R——. He wore a hunted look and told me in a hushed voice exactly the same secrets, which *he* had just had from "T.R." On the way down Pennsylvania Avenue we came across W—— swelling with the same news, and an hour or so later it was all in the evening paper! Mr. Taft was also a free talker and gave outright opinions both of events and of men but did anyone ever see an interview with either Mr. Roosevelt or Mr. Taft that contained anything really new?

So it is to a peculiar degree with Mr. Wilson. I really believe that if every conversation the President has upon public affairs with his intimate advisers were stenographically reported and published, little would be added to our essential knowledge either of the man or of his views. Is not this as it should be in a republic?

What one does get in a direct conversation—and nothing is more valuable in forming an estimate of a man—is a more vivid impression of fundamental personality: a new sense of the real man and his real convictions. And this is peculiarly important in Mr. Wilson's case because no President in recent years has come into direct contact with so few people outside of his official associates. When Mr. Roosevelt was President everybody and his neighbor visited him at the White House; and Mr. Taft was an inveterate traveler and delighted in dinners, receptions, and all kinds of public meetings; but Mr. Wilson, besides being temperamentally of the thoughtful and studious type, has had such problems to meet as no other President has had since Lincoln. With a world in conflagration about him, Mr. Wilson has had to deny many visitors, cancel many appointments to speak, disappoint many important gatherings, and has thus been prevented from coming into direct personal contact with thousands of Americans.

It is curious, the all-of-a-stripeness of men. If you find a man organized, or, indeed, unorganized in one respect, he is likely to be similarly organized or disorganized in other ways. Taft, for example, big, smiling, easy-going, friendly, philosophical, loyal Taft, in his personal characteristics, is singularly of the same quality in his thinking: a laziness in thought, a blur of good humor over all his judgments, the dislike of the comfortable and well-fed man of being intellectually uprooted or disturbed, a want of sharpness in his distinctions and of steadiness in his decisions, a desire as an executive to offend no one, therefore offending everyone, a loyalty to persons often superior to loyalty to principles.

T.R.'s thinking and decisions are also in keeping with his temperament—quick, nervous, irritable, extreme. He loves roughing it intellectually as well as physically, and if his hard-ridden horse sometimes throws and bruises him, so do his ideas. We have always the feeling with him that it is the zest of adventure, the thrill of the game, that engages him rather than the far, hard quest. He rides to ride rather than to arrive. He explores to explore rather than to find a River of Doubt. He has a "bully time" of it in politics, and it is perhaps not immaterial but incidental whether he bags the "square deal," trounces the "malefactors of great wealth," saves water powers, or secures adequate preparedness. We have a feeling that he would have been in the 1916 campaign—in fact we know he could not have been kept out of it—if Belgium had not been raped and America already had a great army or navy; and the issues he would have found would have been equally "fundamental" and supported with an equal fury of emphasis.

So it is with Mr. Wilson. A keen, spare, sharp-cut man, sharp-cut and spare in mind as in features, light on his feet, deft in his movements, a silent, intense worker, a lover of intellectual athletics, delighting in new and strong ideas—he is all of a piece. No blur about him, no heaviness of thought, loyalty to principles always superior to loyalty to persons, he is as different from Mr. Taft as a man could well be.

He is also utterly different from Mr. Roosevelt. He does not have a "bully time" of it in politics, but takes the Presidency hard, with an often painful sense of the hugeness of his task and the greatness of his responsibility. We could never think of T.R. taking any problem to God: why share any of his joys? And if T.R. rides to ride, Woodrow Wilson always rides to arrive. His eye is always on the far, hard quest. He is never irritable, never extreme, but always steady, always quiet, "holding the long purpose like a growing tree."

Thus it becomes quite a different kind of adventure—a conversation with Mr. Wilson compared with a conversation with Mr. Roosevelt. When one comes away from a talk with T.R. he says: "What a wonderful man! How interesting! How amusing! How vital! Surely the greatest man in the world!" But when one comes away from a talk with Mr. Wilson, he says: "What wonderful ideas he has! What mastery of facts! What an understanding of principles! How clear! How trustworthy!"

When Roosevelt speaks he makes us think irresistibly of Roosevelt, but when Wilson speaks he makes us think irresistibly of what he says. When Wilson marched the other day in the preparedness parade at Washington, he contrived to a curious degree to keep people's attention not upon himself, but upon the idea he was symbolizing. It was not the fact that he was marching that impressed the spectators, but that he was marching in a preparedness parade. He kept the idea uppermost.

All men live by selling themselves in one way or another, but Mr. Wilson is a poor salesman of himself. In an age swayed by advertising he is a poor advertiser; and in a nation which forms its opinions largely by reading headlines he is a poor headliner. T.R. was a supreme master in both arts, and he has sold himself at the highest prices to the American people for years. To be a good salesman a man must be supremely interested in what he is trying to sell. Mr. Roosevelt is so interested in himself, while Mr. Wilson is not at all interested in himself. He shrinks from publicity, and the White House since he has been there has yielded mere reluctant trickles of news, while in T.R.'s time it gushed torrents. What Mr. Wilson is trying to sell, what supremely interests him, are ideas, principles, duties; and they are and always have been hard to sell, and the more valuable they are the less people seem to want them. Almost more than anything else people hate being asked to think, and they want to be told of their rights rather than of their duties. He is also trying to sell his record and the record of his party in Congress, and these are at present good, solid wares, not as interesting as a vivid or amusing personality, but sound and stable. If Mr. Wilson, the man, is sold to the American people, it must be by his friends, who know him, who trust him, and who think that kind of a man to be supremely necessary to the nation in such a crisis as this. As for the ideas and principles, Mr. Wilson can sell them on as good terms as any man at this moment living upon God's green footstool, for there is no man who can window-dress them more artfully in words.

I have never talked with any other public man who gave me such an impression of being at every moment in complete command of his entire intellectual equipment, such an impression of alertness, awareness. His face mirrors that eagerness. A new fact, a new aspect of an old situation, a felicitous statement of current opinion, brings to his intent eyes an expression of keen intellectual appetite. He pounces upon ideas half conveyed and consumes them before they are well out of one's mind; and his pounce is sure and accurate. He gets swiftly to your point of view, passes upon the facts that you bring him, and in a few minutes' time has stripped the whole situation to the bare bones of its fundamental aspects, and has rested his conclusions and decisions upon a few simple and elemental principles—and all with an incomparable clearness of statement.

Some critics of Mr. Wilson jeer at this gift of lucid expression; but there is nothing surer in this world than that a man who speaks or writes clearly also thinks clearly. "The style is the man."

Herein lies one of the great sources of the President's power, both in his own party and in the nation. A Congressman who has had occasion to go to the White House several times with a more or less hostile committee told me vividly how Mr. Wilson did it.

"We always come away feeling that we have been convinced, not by Mr. Wilson—certainly not driven or bossed by him—but with the feeling that we are all—President, Congress, and people —in the presence of an irresistible situation. Here are the facts, he says; here are the principles, here are our obligations as Democrats. What are we going to do about it? He has a curious way of making one feel that he, along with all of us, is perfectly helpless before the facts in the case."

Men of power often give the impression of being worked *through* by forces greater than themselves. They are disinterested;

they are concerned in the work they are trying to do rather than in themselves. We sometimes get a strong sidelight on a man's character by observing the qualities he commends in other people. Twice I heard Mr. Wilson, in speaking of certain well-known men, emphasize above all other traits their "disinterestedness." One gets the sense strongly in talking with Mr. Wilson, as in reading his books, that he sees and feels the nation as a living thing, going forward, doing what needs to be done, with himself unimportant save as an instrument. . . .

Now, a man who considers himself an instrument for the accomplishment of certain purposes must have a very clear idea of what those purposes are, and what the forces are which he feels working through him.

One who listens alertly will find that most men have a certain refrain, a certain note often struck, a kind of interpretive chord. As I have listened to Mr. Wilson, it seems to me that this refrain appears with exceeding clearness. I also find it everywhere recurrent in what he has written. In one of his books, containing especially his more recent utterances, I have noted and underlined one word or its equivalents which constantly appears. It seems to be a key word with him, not only in his personal attitude toward life, but in his view of the attitude of the nation toward its problems. This word is "duty." The idea of duty, the duty of the President, the duty of Congress, the duty of the Democratic party, the duty of the nation loom large in everything that Mr. Wilson says or does. He talks indeed about rights also, as he has talked about the rights of the Mexicans to control their own affairs, but when he thinks of America he seems to think first of our duties, afterward of our rights. Mr. Wilson is Scotch Presbyterian in his origin, and I fancy that this point of view, more or less unconscious, is deeply ingrained in his very nature.

During the first half of his administration, in urging the Democratic party to get together, it was the note of collective obligation to keep its promises to the people which was significant above everything else, with the result that no administration in years has placed upon the statute books such a notable body of progressive legislation.

When the European war broke out, however much others might think of the rights of Americans—and Mr. Wilson has not neglected that aspect of the problem, as his public papers show— his first strong desire was that America should do its duty. In his first great utterance, in August, 1914, there is not a word about the rights of Americans or of the American nation, but an expression in the highest and most solemn language of the "proper performance of our duty as the one great nation at peace."

In his attitude toward Mexico he is also constantly impressing on America its duty, its duty, its duty—the duty of the strong toward the weak. And he has shown impatience only with those Americans whose insistence upon their rights as investors in Mexico had blinded them to any sense of the larger duty of the nation. Consider, for example, the President's message to Congress in August, 1914:

"I deem it my duty to speak very frankly of what this government has done and should seek to do in fulfillment of its obligation to Mexico itself, as a friend and neighbor, and to American citizens whose lives and vital interests are daily affected by the distressing conditions which now obtain beyond our southern border. . . . We shall yet prove to the Mexican people that we know how to serve them without first thinking how we shall serve ourselves. . . . It was our duty at least to volunteer our good offices. . . . It was our duty to offer our active assistance. It is now our duty to show what true neutrality will do to enable the people of Mexico to set their affairs in order. . . . We shall triumph as Mexico's friends sooner than we could triumph as her enemies—and how much more handsomely, with how much higher and finer satisfaction of conscience and of honor!"

Duty is here made the keynote of our national policy; and without a sense of this keynote, the essence of the thing to which

Mr. Wilson is bending all his great power, one cannot understand, in all its bigness and its vision, the end which he seeks.

These instances and references could be indefinitely multiplied and anyone can so multiply them by examining Mr. Wilson's utterances and studying his acts. It is by this discipline of duty that he brought the torn Democratic party together and made it an efficient legislative tool, and it is his high sense of the duty of America as the one great and powerful nation at peace that has dictated his policies toward Europe and toward Mexico.

If he seems to be, indeed often is, an opportunist in his attitude toward Mexico, for example, it is because the situation is in flux and must be dealt with tentatively. A man with his eyes less intently fixed upon what he considered the supreme duty of the nation might easily take a short-cut course, and, careless of what really did eventuate, appear far more logical than Mr. Wilson does. It would be easy, for instance, to go to war, for the consideration of the end to be attained would then be lost in the delirious excitement of the means employed. But here in the White House is a man willing to try and fail, try again and fail again, seek this opening, improve that opportunity, and all with consummate patience, because the end to be attained seems so wonderfully well worth attaining.

One other impression of meeting and talking with Mr. Wilson must also be chronicled. Here is a heavily burdened man—after all, a human being, though a President—having to meet fierce and often unreasoning attacks. No President certainly since Lincoln has been confronted with such mountains of perplexities, and none since Lincoln has been so violently attacked both for what he has done and what he has failed to do. None has worked harder or more faithfully. And yet under both the burden of his problems and the attacks upon him one finds him patient and serene. For he is serene, and the atmosphere of the White House is exactly as I have described it: one of quiet confidence. A man less well-fortified within would give a far different impression!

It is a time when events loom large and leaders look small. In all the countries in Europe no man seems big enough for the problems presented, and the cry is for supermen when there are no supermen, but only hard-working, hard-thinking human beings. All leaders have been under furious attack, cabinets have fallen, and ministers have been superseded. It is so easy in times of stress to stand aside and blame the leader for everything. What is impressive in Mr. Wilson is that he is still so strongly master of the situation, still so sure of himself. I was greatly pleased when I heard that Wordsworth's "Happy Warrior" was Mr. Wilson's favorite poem! For it seems to me that here is truly a "generous Spirit . . . whose law is reason; who depends upon that law as on the best of friends," who when he rose "to station of command" rose "by open means," and who, when called upon to face

> Some awful moment to which Heaven has joined
> Great issues, good or bad for human kind—

Keeps with steadiness and serenity the law

> In calmness made, and sees what he foresaw;
> Or if an unexpected call succeed,
> Come when it will, is equal to the need.

With many of the people of this country Mr. Wilson has won about the highest prize that any leader can win in a democracy— higher than personal fame, higher than popular enthusiasm—for millions of people *trust* him.

✪

On the Eve of War

"The night before he [Wilson] asked Congress for a declaration of
war against Germany he sent for me [Frank I. Cobb].* I was late
getting the message somehow and didn't reach the White House till
one o'clock in the morning. 'The old man' was waiting for me,
sitting in his study with the typewriter on his table, where he used
to type his own messages.

"I'd never seen him so worn down. He looked as if he hadn't
slept, and he said he hadn't. He said he was probably going before
Congress the next day to ask a declaration of war, and he'd never
been so uncertain about anything in his life as about that decision.
For nights, he said, he'd been lying awake going over the whole
situation; over the provocation given by Germany, over the probable feeling in the United States, over the consequences to the
settlement and to the world at large if we entered the melee.

"He tapped some sheets before him and said that he had written
a message and expected to go before Congress with it as it stood.
He said he couldn't see any alternative, that he had tried every way
he knew to avoid war. 'I think I know what war means,' he said,

* This conversation almost certainly occurred on March 19, 1917, when
Wilson was wrestling hardest over the issue of war, not on April 2, when
Wilson delivered his war message [ed.].

From the book *Cobb of "The World"* by John L. Heaton. Copyright,
1924, by E. P. Dutton & Co., Inc. Reprinted by permission of the publishers.

and he added that if there were any possibility of avoiding war he wanted to try it. 'What else can I do?' he said. 'Is there anything else I can do?'

"I told him his hand had been forced by Germany, that so far as I could see we couldn't keep out.

"'Yes,' he said, 'but do you know what that means?' He said war would overturn the world we had known; that so long as we remained out, there was a preponderance of neutrality, but that if we joined with the Allies the world would be off the peace basis and onto a war basis.

"It would mean that we should lose our heads along with the rest and stop weighing right and wrong. It would mean that a majority of people in this hemisphere would go war-mad, quit thinking and devote their energies to destruction. The President said a declaration of war would mean that Germany would be beaten and so badly beaten that there would be a dictated peace, a victorious peace.

"'It means,' he said, 'an attempt to reconstruct a peace-time civilization with war standards, and at the end of the war there will be no bystanders with sufficient power to influence the terms. There won't be any peace standards left to work with. There will be only war standards.'

"The President said that such a basis was what the Allies thought they wanted, and that they would have their way in the very thing America had hoped against and struggled against. W.W. was uncanny that night. He had the whole panorama in his mind. He went on to say that so far as he knew he had considered every loophole of escape and as fast as they were discovered Germany deliberately blocked them with some new outrage.

"Then he began to talk about the consequences to the United States. He had no illusions about the fashion in which we were likely to fight the war.

"He said when a war got going it was just war and there weren't two kinds of it. It required illiberalism at home to reinforce the men at the front. We couldn't fight Germany and maintain the ideals of government that all thinking men shared. He said we would try it but it would be too much for us.

"'Once lead this people into war,' he said, 'and they'll forget there ever was such a thing as tolerance. To fight you must be brutal and ruthless, and the spirit of ruthless brutality will enter into the very fiber of our national life, infecting Congress, the courts, the policeman on the beat, the man in the street.' Conformity would be the only virtue, said the President, and every man who refused to conform would have to pay the penalty.

"He thought the Constitution would not survive it; that free speech and the right of assembly would go. He said a nation couldn't put its strength into a war and keep its head level; it had never been done.

"'If there is any alternative, for God's sake, let's take it,' he exclaimed. Well I couldn't see any, and I told him so.

"The President didn't have illusions about how he was going to come out of it, either. He'd rather have done anything else than head a military machine. All his instincts were against it. He foresaw too clearly the probable influence of a declaration of war on his own fortunes; the adulation certain to follow the certain victory, the derision and attack which would come with the deflation of excessive hopes and in the presence of world responsibility. But if he had it to do over again he would take the same course. It was just a choice of evils."

✪

Wilson at Paris

No one who really saw the President in action at Paris, saw what he did in those grilling months of struggle, fired at in front, sniped at from behind—and no one who saw what he had to do after he came home from Europe in meeting the great new problems which grew out of the war—will for a moment belittle the immensity of his task, or underrate his extraordinary endurance, energy, and courage. More than once, there in Paris, going up in the evening to see the President, I found him looking utterly worn out, exhausted, often one side of his face twitching with nervousness. No soldier ever went into battle with more enthusiasm, more aspiration, more devotion to a sacred cause than the President had when he came to Paris; but day after day in those months we saw him growing grayer and grayer, grimmer and grimmer, with the fighting lines deepening in his face.

Here was a man sixty-three years old—a man always delicate in health. When he came into the White House in 1913, he was far from being well. His digestion was poor and he had a serious and painful case of neuritis in his shoulder. It was even the opinion of so great a physician as Dr. Weir Mitchell of Philadelphia that he

From Ray Stannard Baker, *What Wilson Did at Paris* (New York: Doubleday, Page & Company, 1919), pp. 3–11, 88–98. Copyright 1919 by Doubleday, Page & Company; reprinted by permission of Rachel Baker Napier in behalf of the heirs of Ray Stannard Baker.

could probably not complete his term and retain his health. And yet such was the iron self-discipline of the man and such was the daily watchful care of Dr. Grayson that instead of gradually going down under the tremendous tasks of the Presidency in the most crowded moments of our national history, he steadily gained strength and working capacity, until in those months in Paris he literally worked everybody at the Peace Conference to a standstill.

It is so easy and cheap to judge people, even Presidents, without knowing the problems they have to face. So much of the President's aloofness at Paris, so much of his unwillingness to expend energy upon unnecessary business, unnecessary conferences, unnecessary visitors—especially the visitors—was due directly to the determination to husband and expend his too limited energies upon tasks that seemed to him essential.

As I say, he worked everybody at the Peace Conference to a standstill. He worked not only the American delegates, but the way he drove the leisurely diplomats of Europe was often shameful to see. Sometimes he would have two meetings going on at the same time. Once I found a meeting of the Council of "the Big Four" going on in his study, and a meeting of the financial and economic experts—twenty or thirty of them—in full session upstairs in the drawing room—and the President oscillating between the two.

It was he who was always the driver, the initiator, at Paris: he worked longer hours, had more appointments, granted himself less recreation, than any other man, high or low, at the Peace Conference. For he was the central figure there. Everything headed up in him.

Practically all of the meetings of the Council of Four were held in his study in the Place des États-Unis. This was the true Capitol of the Peace Conference; here all the important questions were decided. Everyone who came to Paris upon any mission whatsoever aimed first of all at seeing the President. Representatives of the little, downtrodden nationalities of the earth—from eastern Europe, Asia, and Africa—thought if they could only get at the

President, explain their pathetic ambitions, confess their troubles to him, all would be well.

I remember vividly one such delegation which symbolized the instinctive trust of the smaller nations in America, and their hope in Wilson's leadership. I came into the office one morning and found two as extraordinary figures as ever came to Paris. They were Polish peasants clad in their own homespun natural wool, red-embroidered, with Cossack caps of shaggy black fur. They had with them a Polish priest, who spoke French, to tell what they wanted. It seems that they were from a little pocket settlement of Poles in the mountains of northern Austria, and that in the boundaries that had been set at Paris they were included in the new nation of the Czechoslovaks.

They told, and the priest interpreted, how one of them had heard in his mountain home that the American President who was at Paris had said that people should be free, should have a right to determine how and by whom they were to be governed. He wanted to be in Poland, not in Czechoslovakia, and so he had set out to walk to Paris to tell the President so. As soon as he got out of his own native mountains he lost his way—so they told me—and turned aside to inquire of a Polish sheepherder. "He was a man," said the priest, "who knew the stars, and the way to go." This sheepherder, when he heard the traveler tell his story, said that he, too, "wanted to be free" (as the priest expressed it) and came along with him to watch the stars and point out the way to go.

They walked some hundred or more miles into Warsaw where their story attracted the attention of a patriotic Polish society, which sent them on to Paris. And they came down the boulevards straight to the Crillon Hotel to find President Wilson. They actually did find him. I saw them—the peasant and the astronomer who knew the stars, and the priest who talked for them—going up the carpeted stairs of the President's house and into his book-walled study. And I could smell the very odor of their thick woven wool garments, redolent of the soil, in that unfamiliar place.

I think that no one who was in Paris will ever forget the way in which the people of the little oppressed nations of the world turned to America for leadership—or staked their passionate hope upon the principles of justice laid down by President Wilson. And it now appears that there are those in America who would shake off every claim to such leadership because it involves new duties and responsibilities!

Well, the President saw and heard scores of such foreign delegations; he received patiently the representatives of many organizations of workingmen, businessmen, journalists, women; he saw groups of Jews, Irish, Armenians, Poles, and I don't know how many others; he labored day after day with the disputatious experts of all the delegations; he attended innumerable committee meetings.

In addition to meeting all the problems that Mr. Lloyd George, M. Clemenceau, and Signor Orlando had to meet, he took upon himself, as his especial task, the chairmanship of the League of Nations Commission which, in order not to interrupt the regular sessions of the Council of Ten or the Council of Four, often met in the evening, with the discussions sometimes extending far beyond midnight. It was one of the hardest-worked commissions at the conference.

I saved the list of the President's appointments for a single day (May 16, 1919), on which there happened to be no meeting of the Council of Four. It gives a vivid glimpse of his activities. Here it is:

11:00 A.M. Prince Charoon, and the Siamese Delegation at the Peace Conference.
11:30 " Dr. A. Markoff, and the Carpatho-Russian Committee, to present the situation in Carpatho-Russia.
11:45 " M. Olivier, president of the National Union of Railway Men of France, to explain the humanitarian and sanitary program of the National Union of French and Belgian Railway Men.

12:00 M.   M. J. Jacob, president of the Celtic Circle of Paris, to
            present an anthology of national bards and poets.
12:15 P.M. Dr. Juan Antonio Buero, and M. Jacob Verela Acevedo,
            delegates to the Peace Conference from Uruguay.
12:30 "   Turkhan Pasha, president of the present government of
            Albania, to present the claims of Albania.
12:45 "   Señor Villegas, ex-Secretary of State of Chili, Minister of
            Chili at Rome.
 2:15 "   Dr. Edward Benes, and M. Kramar, to discuss the prob-
            lem of Silesia and the Teschen Coal Basin.
 2:30 "   M. Damour, French Deputy, chairman of the committee
            to explain the plans for the erection of a statue at the
            mouth of the Gironde River to commemorate the ar-
            rival of American troops in France.
 2:45 "   A delegation from the Parliament of Kouban in northern
            Caucasia.
 3:00 "   The Archbishop of Trebizond, M. Chrysanthos.
 3:15 "   Governor Manning of South Carolina.
 3:30 "   M. Joseph Reinach, of the Paris *Figaro*.

I recall asking, when I received this list of appointments: "Is
this all?"

No, it was not all; he had had guests in for luncheon and he had
completed on that day his important message to the extraordinary
session of Congress which he had called to meet on May 20. This
was a document of some thirty-five hundred words and he had
written it himself on his typewriter. It must not be forgotten, in
thinking of the President's task at Paris, that he was constantly
required to face problems and make decisions regarding affairs at
home, some of them requiring much time and thought.

Besides all of these things he was called upon as no other man
of any nation at the conference was called upon—almost forced—
to attend public functions of various sorts, to make speeches, to
visit neighboring countries; and he was often bitterly censured
because he did not do more of this, did not visit more frequently
the devastated districts of France, did not review this parade, or
accept that exhausting hospitality. . . .

How the President bore up under the continual strain of his task at this time with all the other demands upon him incident to his great position, is truly a mystery. Sometimes when I went up to see him, in the evening, he looked utterly beaten, worn out; but the next morning he would appear refreshed and eager to go on with the fight. I fancied sometimes that he had discovered the mysterious formula for unlocking the hidden inner energies, about which Professor William James wrote so persuasively in his essay on the "Energies of Men." In these days, although he occupied the very center of the world's great stage, with all humanity watching every move he made, listening for every word he said, he lived almost the life of an anchorite. For days, there in late April, he saw almost nobody not intimately connected with the actual business of the conference. He had no social life at all, no recreation, scarcely any exercise. Sometimes in the evening I used to find him in the study of his house: a dark, richly furnished room looking out upon a little patch of walled garden with an American sentinel pacing up and down the passageway. A prisoner could not have been more watchfully guarded! But the prison cell itself was a charming place. The French owner of the house had been an art lover and there hung in this room a number of rare old pictures: an interesting Rembrandt, a Delacroix, an Hobbema, several Goyas. I wondered sometimes what Rembrandt would have made of "A Sitting of the Four" if he had been there to paint it! It was a curious room, this study, seeming to have only one entrance, but one day I saw the President step to the back of the room and open and go through what appeared to be a solid, well-filled bookcase into a passageway leading to his bedroom beyond. It was a concealed door cunningly painted to look like a case filled with books.

Mrs. Wilson's sitting room was opposite the President's study, with a small reception room between, and her sunny window opened also on the little grassy court; and above the wall, across the street, one could look into the upper windows of the house occupied by Mr. Lloyd George. Some day there will be written an account of the incalculable help and comfort that Mrs. Wilson was to the President in these trying days. In every difficult situation in Europe, Mrs. Wilson comported herself with fine dignity and with genuine simplicity and graciousness of manner.

The President got almost no exercise during this last hard spurt in April, for there was literally no time for it. Occasionally he would take a short automobile ride in the Bois with Mrs. Wilson, sometimes a little brisk walk with Admiral Grayson. And he would stand by the open window, now and then, in such moments as he could catch, and breathe deeply. He did everything possible to get every ounce of energy out of his bodily and mental machine, for his daily struggle.

I heard the assertion solemnly made the other day that the trouble with the President at Paris was that he would not see the experts of the delegation; or would not hear all sides of the case. The fault, if any, was really upon the other side. He tried too hard to get every angle, every point of view; he was tempted to wait too long to be absolutely sure of facts upon which he must base his decisions. This, throughout his whole career, has been his inclination—his fault, if you like. Mr. Thomas W. Lamont, who was one of the financial experts of the commission, met this accusation vigorously in a recent public statement.

"I hear it repeated," he said, "that he was unwilling to take counsel with his delegation. That is untrue. He constantly and earnestly sought the advice of his associates."

Indeed, it was he, beyond any other man, who wanted all the facts presented to the Council. Two such cases, among many, come to my memory. Both the Italians and the Japanese, of course, had seats in the Supreme Council of the five great powers and naturally could keep their own claims always before their associates. Under such circumstances the Jugoslavs and the Chinese might have had a hard time getting a proper consideration of their cases. But the President urged the fullest hearing of the Jugoslavs, and they got it, even though Orlando declined to be present at the sitting. In the same way the President stood for a full hearing of the Chinese by the Council of Ten; and a notable presentation of the Chinese case was given by Mr. Wellington Koo. On the other hand, it was Mr. Wilson beyond any other, who was most anxious to have the Japanese—the silent partners of the conference—express their views upon all the difficult issues.

Last Years

To the zero hour Woodrow Wilson regarded himself as the spiritual leader of a cause only temporarily lost. Despite his shattered health, he never completely abandoned the hope that he might again become the standard-bearer of his party. Under no circumstance would he permit his intimates to commit him to any other candidacy. And he confidently expected to dictate the paramount issues in the coming Presidential campaign [i.e., 1924], which explains much of the nervous anxiety of the past fall and early winter among Democratic candidates and chieftains, particularly those practical folks who felt that the debacle of 1920 had provided a right decent burial for the League of Nations.

It was my privilege to spend the afternoons of October 23 and December 7 last [1923] with Mr. Wilson at his Washington home. On the occasion of these visits he made clear his belief that the liberals of the world were looking to him to lead them. Whatever historians may do, there can never be a doubt of his own intense conviction that his place was to fight what he was fond of terming the spiritual battles of humanity and democracy. It was a passion

From James Kerney, "Last Talks with Woodrow Wilson," *Saturday Evening Post,* CXCVI (March 29, 1924), pp. 3–4. Reprinted with permission from *The Saturday Evening Post.* Copyright 1924 The Curtis Publishing Company.

with him. I had suggested that, in view of his physical breakdown, he might find an easy way to emerge from his retirement and give effectual voice to his ideas by standing for the United States Senate from New Jersey—not a particularly new thought.

We talked the situation over from all angles—the fact that Governor Silzer, strongest vote-getter among New Jersey Democrats, did not want to run for Senator; the possibility that the independent newspapers and state forces that had put over Wilson's first political program, and stood by him in his later fights, would line up again; the chance that even the solidly intrenched party machine would accept him. At our meeting on October 23 he asked me to go to New York and canvass the ground with his two confidential advisers—Bernard M. Baruch and Norman Davis.

But while appearing ready to consider the Senate as a remotely possible outlet for leadership, his thoughts seemed plainly elsewhere. He was bitter in his expressions of contempt for the Senate itself, and at one point he said, with a flash of the old-time vigor, "There is only one place, you know, where I could be sure of effectively asserting that leadership." That was the nearest I ever heard him come to a declaration of candidacy, but he did repeatedly emphasize his determination to prevent any temporizing with his League policies. The Democratic candidate, he declared, would not be agreed upon until the national convention was two or three days old; meanwhile he expected to lay before the delegates a program of principles that would bring vindication at the polls. There was to be no backing down. He was full of hope about giving his views to the world. It was impossible to pin him down to writing anything, however. Frequently he spoke of finding a way of assisting liberal thought; but, aside from the November radio speech, he apparently did nothing.

Upon leaving the S Street home in the afternoon of October 23, I promptly put into written form the substance of what the former

President had said. He had been exceedingly generous in his expressions of friendship and declared that he was baring his soul to me.

"I am going to try to look at myself as though I did not exist," he added; "to consider the whole thing in an impersonal way. From the messages I get I realize that I am everywhere regarded as the foremost leader of the liberal thought of the world, and the hopes and aspirations of that liberal thought should find some better place of expression than in the Senate. There is only one place, you know, where I could be sure of effectively asserting that leadership. Outside of the United States, the Senate does not amount to a damn; and inside the United States the Senate is mostly despised; they haven't had a thought down there in fifty years.

"You know and I know that I have a temper, and if I was to go to the Senate I should get into a row with that old Lodge, who no longer counts for anything. As I have remarked before of him, I'd rather be a dead dead man than a dead live man. The Senate would hardly provide the place for liberal leadership that the world is seeking so sadly. Think of the people of Poland and of Czechoslovakia and the other countries to whom we gave freedom—they know that they owe their very national existence to me, and they are looking to me to lead them. When I think of that fine old fellow, Jan Smuts, for whom I have the greatest affection, and the others of liberal tendencies who are looking to me, I feel that I should do my part. My present political advisers are Bernard Baruch and Norman Davis, and I am going to ask you to see them in New York and talk the situation over and get the benefit of their views. Try to see them together. Perhaps we can yet find some way out."

We talked of many other things. When I entered the library he was seated in a big chair by the fireside. He was most cordial in his words of welcome, but remarked sadly, "I'm helpless, Kerney; this left side is gone." His spirit appeared to be badly shot that day. The morning papers had printed official denials of one of those periodical news-ticker rumors of his death. I think the visit of David Lloyd George, on the previous afternoon, had been a bit of a disappointment too. According to the former President, about all that Lloyd George appeared to want to hear was a repetition of some of the limericks with which Wilson had regaled the European statesmen at Paris and Versailles. When I shifted the conversation to old times in New Jersey, his mood mellowed a bit and he got a smile out of the news that James R. Nugent, master mechanic of the steamroller that had nominated him for Governor back in 1910, had once again captured the Essex County Democratic organization.

"Nugent is a strange fellow, and though we had some powerful disagreements I always had a feeling of regard for him," Mr. Wilson declared.

He was keenly interested in the coal and road and public utility fights that Silzer, as Governor, had been making in New Jersey.

"Silzer is splendidly equipped for public service; he has vision and courage, and those veto messages of last winter were models," he added.

When it came time for his afternoon automobile ride I took my leave, assuring him that I would go to New York at an early date and talk over the Senatorship, as well as the situation in general, with Baruch and Davis.

"I hope God will bless you and your family with good health and every happiness," he said as we shook hands in parting.

During the thirteen years since Wilson had come conspicuously into public life, I had as editor of the *Trenton Times*—from a friendly seat on the sidelines—been given an occasional glimpse of most of the confidential advisers. I doubt if any ever had his complete confidence; it was not the Wilson way. Not that there was no affectionate warmth for those with whom he came into personal relationship. At Princeton he had been both the best-loved and best-hated member of the faculty. In his public career it was the same.

By nature Wilson was a lonely man, a dreamer, with the type of intellect that found it difficult to tolerate ordinary mortals. His supreme self-confidence was perhaps his biggest handicap, as well as his most outstanding virtue. His habit was to rely upon his own dominating personality and power of persuasion to put things across. It was his lack of flexibility, of accommodation of mind, that led to much of the bitterness and disappointment that came to him in life.

Few, if any, public men thrown into intimate association with Wilson made the whole political distance with him. Harvey, Watterson, Smith, Nugent, House, Lansing—all fell by the way-side. Joseph P. Tumulty, worshipful secretary, seeing no blemish in his idol, retained the favor longest and, outside of the immediate family and one or two old university friends like Cleveland Dodge and Stockton Axson, was best loved. Dr. Grayson of course became a part of the family life.

Tumulty, the playboy, reveling in the dramatics of it all, had given a dozen years of practical political experience, unstinted devotion and joyous laughter to the great mind that so often found itself impatiently battling with a world that would not see freedom the Wilson way. But the ill-starred Tumulty book, about which Wilson appeared to be quite informed even if he had never read it, coupled with the seemingly harmless, if unauthorized, message of felicitation that Tumulty carried to the testimonial dinner to James M. Cox in New York, completely barred all further personal contact. Friends vainly tried to patch it up.

The thought that the complimentary message might be regarded throughout the country as an endorsement of Cox was too much for Wilson. He was not for Cox, and was very definitely not ready even to appear to be committing himself to any of the candidates for the Presidency, although he frankly told me that

"Cox was a very brave man to take up the League of Nations fight in 1920." Despite the estrangement, Wilson never lost his admiration for Tumulty's public experience and service. A few days after he had asked me to go to New York and talk with Baruch and Davis about the wisdom of his considering the Senate possibility, I received a letter suggesting Tumulty for the Senatorship as a man of exceedingly wide and varied experience in both our state and national political life, and one who would help to make the reactionaries see that we were living in new times and under new conditions.

November first, the day after I received the above-mentioned letter, Mr. Baruch took me to the home of Mr. Davis in New York, where we spent several hours in discussing the whole situation. The feeling of both men was that the former President would be merely hurrying his death in becoming a candidate for any office. That had been my own feeling as I walked downtown from the Wilson home in Washington. It was finally agreed that Baruch and Davis should each write frankly to Wilson, and that, after the lapse of a period of time, I should go back and see him. The suggestion of Tumulty or Daniels had been made, but was not practical. Neither had lived in New Jersey for a decade. President Wilson had named Professor Daniels, a Princeton man, to the Interstate Commerce Commission.

When I went back to see Mr. Wilson, December 7, he was in excellent spirits. His eye was bright, his mind fairly flashed with sharp things, and altogether he was full of that snap and pep that characterized the earlier days at Trenton and Washington. He reclined on a big steamer chair, wrapped comfortably in a blanket, on the upper sun porch of his home. It was balmy as springtime in Paris and we chatted for nearly an hour. He felt that the reception that had been given his Armistice Day radio speech showed the swing of the pendulum back in his direction—and he did not hesitate to say so. When I reminded him that there was quite an international furor over his radio reference to the "sinister climax" of France and Italy's having "made wastepaper of the Treaty of Versailles," he fired back in a spirited voice, "I should like to see Germany clean up France, and I should like to meet Jusserand and tell him that to his face." He was plainly irritated at the French politicians; none among them, save Loucheur, he felt had told him the entire truth. Stanley Baldwin's defeat was a good thing not only for England but for its effect on Poincaré, "who is a bully," he added.

"His master's voice has spoken," was his breezy comment on President Coolidge's message to Congress.

The message did not breathe one human hope, he said, but it would insure the nomination of Coolidge by the big-business crowd. The American farmer was not going to be fooled again on the European question; the farmer, he felt, was now fully aware that our unsettled foreign relations were playing havoc with business at home.

Of the administration's World Court idea, he said, "They don't know where they're drifting; Hughes is at sea and they have no program." The Republican stupidity, he declared, would give the Democrats their great chance and he meant to see to it that there was no surrender to "the pocketbook brigade."

He was much disappointed at the enthusiastic way so many Democrats appeared to be abandoning principles and ideals in their anxiety to get their income taxes reduced.

"Wealth has its place," he said; "but it should not be the master; it should be made to serve the same as the rest of us." And he proceeded to express his complete disgust at the public indifference toward low moral standards in government. He always despised the traffic in prestige by those who had won the great prizes of governmental office. There is no secret about the resentment he felt at officials who resigned before their time was out to go after the big fees. Though such procedure might be within the law, he was strongly opposed to it on ethical grounds. He would not yield even to the pressure of those who felt he might with absolute propriety accept some adequate compensation for his writings, as Roosevelt had done. His prestige was not for sale in any market.

It was an impossible task to pin him down to writing for publication. He did practically none of it after he got into official life. There was a great deal of discussion between us, on that last December afternoon, regarding the method by which he was going to put over his program for political regeneration, but he reached no decision.

And then came the Christmas holidays and the January visit of the national committee—and the end. He never got a chance to find the way of putting into concrete form the great dreams he was dreaming in his closing years. He died fully convinced that the whole world was shifting his way.

For me, who had seen him start so buoyantly on his political career, following his battle to democratize Princeton, the recollection of his cheerful spirit on that December afternoon is especially pleasant. And when the eye of Joe Tumulty falls on this for the first time it will bring pleasure to him.

"That was a very handsome thing, Governor, you said about Tumulty in your letter," I told Mr. Wilson after we had discussed the impracticability of his being a candidate himself for the United States Senatorship.

"It's the way I felt; Tumulty would make them all sit up and take notice; he could render the country fine service in the Senate," was the gracious reply.

We talked, too, of other days in New Jersey, and he laughingly repeated an oft-expressed belief that anyone who was in politics and couldn't learn all the tricks of the game in short order in New Jersey had better seek some other field of activity.

He was much interested in a recent speech that I had heard Alexander Meiklejohn, former president of Amherst, deliver at the Nassau Club, at Princeton, in which the faculty of his old university got some rather refreshingly frank views on the relationship of alumni and trustees to educators.

"There are many splendid fellows in the Princeton faculty; but they are allowed no freedom of thought," Mr. Wilson remarked with a tone of bitter sadness in his voice. And he added:

"Candidly, Kerney, if I had a son I wouldn't know where to send him for a liberal education in America."

Before I retired he recited a dozen or more limericks. This one of his own, that he had put together to amuse—or perhaps shock—a rather prim woman friend, he repeated with considerable glee:

> There was a young girl from Missouri
> Who took her case to the jury;
>   She said, "Car ninety-three
>   Ran over my knee."
> But the jury said, "We're from Missouri!"

And he got a lot of fun out of repeating the revised version of the old Massachusetts limerick about where the "Lodges speak only to Cabots and the Cabots speak only to God."

"You recall," he said, "how that family of Kabotskis in Philadelphia tried to change the name to Cabot, and how the Cabots went to court for an injunction, and so the limerick had to be made over."

And then, with a merry twinkle, he repeated the revision:

> Here's to Massachusetts,
> The land of the bean and the cod,
> Where the Lodges can't speak to the Cabots
> Because the Cabots speak Yiddish, begob!

There was some yarning, and when I rose to go he cordially urged me to "come back soon." It was my good fortune to have enjoyed a most happy relationship with him from the beginning. His letters always had a great charm of expression, and in matters of etiquette he was most punctilious.

Though his mind never appeared to dim, he was necessarily a cloistered shut-in during the last years of his life. His days were prolonged by the devoted sheltering from the public provided by

Mrs. Wilson and her brother, John Randolph Bolling, who gave up his personal business to act as secretary. Everything was done to guard Woodrow Wilson against the least possible irritation or annoyance, and to conserve his strength. No man ever ended his days in more considerate and loving surroundings.

CHARLES SEYMOUR ⊗

Wilson and His Contributions

Toward the close of Woodrow Wilson's campaign for re-election to the Presidency of the United States, at a moment when prospects seemed unpromising, he remarked: "As compared with the verdict of the next twenty-five years, I do not care a peppercorn about the verdict of 1916." When those twenty-five years had passed, the verdict, if taken, would have been blurred by our intervention in the Second World War. How far has the situation been clarified at the present moment, thirty-two years after Wilson's death, one hundred years after his birth? In the case of Abraham Lincoln, the perspective of far less elapsed time authorized his admission to the Valhalla of American greatness. The same is true, with varying emphasis, of the Founding Fathers of the republic. But since the death of Lincoln, no clear-cut agreement on immortal greatness in the case of any American President has been achieved.

The claims of Wilson to inclusion in the select group cannot be summarily brushed aside. The significance of the reforms he advocated in vital phases of American life is hardly disputed. The nation has soberly accepted the purposes and the policies which at

From Charles Seymour, "Woodrow Wilson in Perspective," *Foreign Affairs*, XXXIV (January 1956), pp. 175–186. Reprinted by special permission from *Foreign Affairs*. Copyright by the Council on Foreign Relations, Inc., New York.

the time that he first urged them aroused a spirit of bitter controversy. This is true of his educational leadership and of the legislative program of his first term as President of the United States.
The tide of history has made it true of the last phase, Wilson's
heroic effort to bring the United States into a system of international cooperation. With little dissent, Americans have come to
take it for granted that the counterpart of the League, the United
Nations, is to be what Allen Dulles has called "our workshop of
peace." Whatever the rebuffs at Princeton and in the United States
Senate, succeeding years have vindicated his vision and his policy.

Thus it is eminently fitting that as political passions have cooled
and personal prejudice softened, fresh consideration should be
given to the position in American history that belongs to Woodrow
Wilson. The verdict of public opinion as well as of the historian
has not yet been rendered in unmistakable form. In what category
and at what level is he finally to be placed?

The importance of Wilson as educational leader has become
definitely established with the passing of the years. That leadership
has not attracted the public attention in like degree with his direction of the movement for international organization. But in itself,
and if he had never entered politics, it would have assured him
permanent distinction. He brought an educational ideal to the
college world at a moment when Princeton and the nation most
needed it. It was not original with him, but there was no one who
expressed it so clearly and persuasively. His courage in the rejection of the free elective system was matched by his insistence upon
teaching quality which would stimulate the student to sincere
interest in and positive enjoyment of study. Thus the main circus
was to regain its dominance over the extracurricular side shows.
His preceptorial plan was only one of various methods by which
the curiosity and intellectual effort of the student might be
aroused. But it caught the imagination of the academic world.
The enthusiasm of the young preceptors aroused their colleagues
in other institutions. The power of Wilson's provocative arguments

for the serious values of college life was infectious. Hence the influence of the Princeton experience served impressively in the general recrudescence of literary and intellectual interest on the American campus.

The controversies which Wilson encountered at Princeton would doubtless have been accepted by most college executives as an inevitable irritation incidental to the office. What seemed to him as defeat, however, coincided with the opportunity to enter politics, his early dream. Thus began, with his success in New Jersey and his astounding advance to the Presidency of the United States, the second phase of his public service. As at Princeton, the earlier aspects of his national political leadership were characterized by almost unbroken success. Indeed, no period of his career since his teaching days has aroused so little controversy and so much praise among historians. They are agreed upon the courage and skill with which he translated an ambitious program of reform into legislation.

In his formulation of the principles of the New Freedom, as well as in his successful demand upon Congress for their immediate political application, Wilson closely approached his own ideals of leadership as laid down in his essay of 1890. His sensitive ear caught the tone of national needs and the trend of popular hopes, which were given form and direction by his persuasive rhetoric. The program was progressive in its farewell to *laissez faire;* it was conservative in its antisocialistic insistence that the authority of government should be used not for the operation, but for the liberation of business. Governor [Adlai] Stevenson points out that "he taught us to distinguish between governmental action that takes over the functions formerly discharged by individuals and governmental action that restores opportunity for individual action." Hence the significant subtitle of his collected campaign speeches: "A Call for the Emancipation of the Generous Energies of a People." He sought in the national arena the equality of opportunity which he had enjoined upon Princeton, the enlargement of the frontiers of freedom which was to be the watchword of his international crusade.

The legislation of the first two years of his Presidency dealt with crucial and contentious issues: the tariff, currency reform, the establishment of the Federal Trade Commission, the Clayton Anti-Trust Act. Wilson's success in achievement in the face of bitter opposition astounded his contemporaries. "This man who was regarded as a pedagogue, a theorist," said Chauncey Depew, "is accomplishing the most astounding practical results."

Of greater historical importance than any contemporary estimate is the almost complete endorsement, over the years, of Wilson's reform program, one that went far toward creating a new social and economic atmosphere. The Federal Reserve is universally taken for granted as the pediment of our national financial structure. The use of federal authority to assure competitive conditions in trade has become a permanent aspect of our economic life. Public opinion has come to accept emancipation of labor, in its organization for the betterment of working conditions, from the restrictions designed to control monopolistic tendencies of capital. The solid permanence of Wilson's legislative achievement is impressive.

The march of events has brought it about that Wilson's position in history would be determined not by the contribution he made to American legislation, important as that was, but rather by the role he played on the international stage. There were three well-defined acts in the drama which began with the outbreak of the European war in August, 1914. The first covered the period of American neutrality, the second that of the active participation of the United States in the war, the third that of the Peace Conference and its aftermath. Wilson's attitude and tactics underwent considerable change during the course of these three periods. But from beginning to end his main purpose was not altered. He was determined to bring the conscience and the power of America into a cooperative effort that would everywhere secure the liberty of all peoples.

Whether as a neutral or belligerent or a peace commissioner, Wilson looked upon himself as leader in a crusade for international freedom.

A sense of responsibility to the rest of the world underlay his policy of determined neutrality. His emotions boiled with protest at the suggestion that he chose neutrality merely as the road to safety. It was imposed upon us, rather, in fulfillment of our duty as the only great neutral at peace, "the one people holding itself ready to play a part of impartial mediation and speak the counsels of peace and accommodation, not as a partisan, but as a friend." His insistence was constant, and today it is recognized as sincere, that we would serve better by remaining outside the conflict. His determination to protect the rights of America against the attacks of the German submarines and the infringements of the British blockade led him finally to espouse the movement for national preparedness. But his call for military armament stressed not merely our rights, but our responsibility for the salvation of the equipoise of the world and "the redemption of the affairs of mankind."

Hence his persistent eagerness in the search for effective methods of mediation, and his constant encouragement to Colonel House in the effort to discover some basis for a compromise peace. Wilson's personal sympathy for the cause of the Entente Allies did not at any time during the period of our neutrality disturb his conviction that such a peace would prove the only sure basis of a permanent settlement. This conviction was at its firmest and clearest as he came to discuss specifically conditions essential to international security, immediately before the break with Germany, in January of 1917. His public suggestion of a "peace without victory" proved offensive to the belligerents and a diplomatic impossibility. But Wilson was quite right in maintaining that a victor's terms imposed upon the vanquished would be "accepted in humiliation, under duress . . . and would leave a sting, a resentment, a bitter memory upon which terms of peace would rest, not permanently, but only as upon quicksand." The quality of Wilson's foresight was amply borne out in the years that followed the Peace Conference and led to the Hitler regime.

There are few who would suggest today that our interests called for intervention in the war previous to the declaration of the intensive German submarine campaign. On the other hand, the band of critics who in later years assailed Wilson as responsible for unnecessary and ultimately disastrous participation in the war has diminished to the vanishing point. That criticism was most strident twenty years ago. It was stimulated by the sense of betrayal that captured American liberals after the Peace Conference as well as by the ill-documented propaganda emanating from the Nye Commission and culminating in the neutrality legislation of the mid-thirties. But it was short-lived. Even those who today believe that only a compromise peace would have provided the base for a permanent settlement admit that Wilson's hand was forced and that the Germans left him no alternative but to enter the war.

Contemporary criticism of the process by which a peaceful, ill-prepared nation was transformed into a fighting machine has been replaced by enthusiastic recognition of the quality of Wilson's leadership in the war. The unity of national effort which he inspired made possible the astounding contribution of American manpower, finance and supplies which turned the tide of battle in Europe. But his outstanding demonstration of leadership lay in the war of ideas. Inevitably the attitude of the President toward the belligerents was radically altered by our own belligerency. He could no longer imply that the war aims on either side were the same. It was not difficult for him to frame his indictment against Germany as an international criminal since he had been profoundly shocked, in a personal sense, by the declaration of submarine warfare. Against such a criminal it was necessary to use force without stint or limit. Henceforth he was unwilling to accept any peace except one based upon the absolute defeat of German militarism.

While Wilson as war leader cast his denunciatory and destructive thunderbolts against the German government, he did not fail to stress constructively the ideals of his crusade for freedom, which he inherited from the period of neutrality and which he led on behalf of all peoples. In his Flag Day address of June 14, 1917, perhaps in itself the outstanding example of his wartime rhetoric, he drew the distinction between the "military masters of Germany [who] denied us the right to be neutral" and the German people, "themselves in the grip of the same sinister power that has . . . stretched its ugly talons out and drawn blood from us." He went on to reiterate his ultimate war aims: "This is the People's War, a war for freedom and justice and self-government amongst all the nations of the world, a war to make the world safe for the peoples who live upon it . . . the German peoples themselves included."

So also in his speech of the Fourteen Points, Wilson forged a weapon of psychological warfare at the same time that he drafted a charter of peace. The address failed in its primary purpose of dissuading Russia from negotiations with the enemy. But it drove a deeper wedge between the German government and people and it presented the latter with the possibilities of an attractive program once their hopes of military victory faded. Germany was offered a place of equality and a guarantee of friendship, "if she is willing to associate herself with us and the other peace-loving nations of the world in covenants of justice and law and fair dealing." Small wonder that when they were confronted with an imminent military collapse, the Germans turned to Wilson, invoking the Fourteen Points and the succeeding speeches couched in similar terms.

Wilson's program as an instrument of political warfare thus achieved resounding success. It became a determining factor in Allied military victory in 1918. It gave to Wilson himself a moral position of such strength that willy-nilly the British and French

leaders in their negotiations with House were compelled to endorse
that program. But the Fourteen Points, a powerful weapon of war,
were not so well fitted to serve as the design for an international
peace settlement. They were at once too general in their statement
of abstract principles and too specific in various geographical
details. Furthermore, the very success of Wilson's psychological
campaign enforced the nationalistic aspirations of the European
peoples and thus raised powerful opposition to his international
ideals.

Wilson went to the Peace Conference pledged to the fulfillment
of a threefold and interlocking concept: the liberation of peoples,
justice for all without distinction, the assurance of peace through
international organization. In his mind, freedom and justice out-
weighed in their importance the assurance of peace; he always
believed that "the right is more precious than peace." But it was
clear that an organized system of security would be essential to the
maintenance of a regime of freedom and justice. All three principles
must be worked out together in a world-wide association of nations:
"A universal dominion of right by such a concert of free peoples as
shall bring peace and safety to all nations and make the world
itself at last free."

Wilson's chief difficulty lay not so much in the opposition of
Allied leaders in Paris, for few would dare openly to oppose such
ideals, as in the inherent difficulty of applying general principles to
concrete issues. For lack of an explicit program, there was at Paris
a high degree of improvisation and of confusion in the effort to
solve specific problems in the light of abstractions which were
difficult to define.

The recurrent leitmotif of Wilson's policy lay in his ideal of
freedom, whether of the individual or of the national group. But
this ideal he found it impossible to formulate at Paris in terms that
might find exact expression in an international agreement. The
principles of self-government were rather vaguely considered in
nineteenth-century concepts, without any clear attempt to reinter-

pret them in contemporary terms or in the light of political and
industrial conditions of Central and Southeastern Europe. The
doctrine of self-determination, expressive of national freedom,
Wilson soon discovered to be an untrustworthy guide, incapable of
universal application. How was he to decide the validity of conflict-
ing aspirations? Linguistic statistics often proved as unreliable a
criterion as the rhetoric of partisan leaders. In various areas he
found the principle of self-determination to be in clear conflict
with other Wilsonian doctrines. It would seem to justify the
separation of the German Sudetenland from Bohemia, an obvious
disaster to the Czechoslovak state, itself founded upon the principle of self-determination. Its strict application would have cut in
two an economic entity such as the Klagenfurt Basin.

In the approach to these and similar problems Wilson hoped for
guidance from the application of the principle of justice, which he
had stressed equally as an essential foundation of a liberating and
a lasting peace. "It must be a justice that seeks no favorites and
knows no standards but the equal rights of the several peoples
concerned. No special or separate interest of any single nation or
any group of nations can be made the basis of any part of the
settlement which is not consistent with the common interest of
all." As a principle this seemed indisputable.

But when he came to cases at Paris he discovered that there was
a conflict of rights as well as of interests. Every government was
bound to feel that justice to its own people demanded a protection
of national security that often could be achieved only at the
expense of another. Even the impartially-minded Americans could
not with any confidence apply the principle of justice to specific
problems. Crossing to Europe on the *George Washington,* Wilson
had said to the members of The Inquiry: "Tell me what's right and
I'll fight for it. Give me a guaranteed position." But whatever
position they might try to guarantee on the basis of justice, a case
could be found with which to dispute it. How did the justice of the
Polish claim to the Corridor compare with the injustice done to

Germany in its establishment? Was the separation of the Saar from the Reich a justifiable reparation for the wanton damage inflicted by German troops on the coal mines of Lens and Valenciennes? As Wilson met Allied leaders day after day, despite the personal irritation of debate, his own attitude toward the strict application of the principle of justice became more fluid.

Wilson's expanding appreciation of the inexorable realities of European politics was manifest in his changed outlook upon the problem of security. This is not to imply that he ever wavered in his conviction that the old system was bankrupt and that the new must be based upon the principle of collective security as expressed in the League of Nations. To that case he devoted his most impassioned efforts. At the opening of the conference it seemed doubtful whether he could withstand pressure for postponement of the League in favor of the "practical" aspects of the settlement; whether, also, he could secure incorporation of the Covenant as the first and essential portion of the treaty with Germany and the others to follow. His triumph was clear-cut. The League became the cornerstone of the treaties. It would serve, Wilson believed, not merely to safeguard the peace but to correct the inequities that were bound to creep into any settlement.

But in the intimate discussions of the Council of Four he came to realize the justified anxiety of the French as to security and the validity of their demand for special guarantees of protection, at least until the League had demonstrated its effective authority. One must read the recently published notes of Professor Mantoux[1] in order to appreciate the emotional and the logical force of the appeal from Clemenceau. The latter's concept of "strategic security," based upon a demilitarized Rhineland and the fortified bastion of Bohemia in the hands of the Czechs, was recognized by Wilson not as a substitute for but as a regional supplement to

---

[1] Paul Mantoux, *Les Délibérations du Conseil des Quartre* (*24 mars–28 juin 1919*) (Paris: Éditions du Centre National de la Recherche Scientifique, 1955), 2 vols.

collective security. And Wilson was further willing to buttress the defense of France by the agreement that the United States would join with Great Britain, in case of attack by Germany, to defend the French frontier.

These departures from ideological perfection have been pictured as constituting a moral and political surrender by Wilson. But he was indebted to Clemenceau for his acquiescence in the League of Nations and he had to acknowledge that conditions in Europe went far to justify the latter's policy. Indeed, that policy, properly implemented, might have sufficed to contain Hitler. The same sort of defense can be offered in behalf of various other compromises that Wilson accepted. They were, in his opinion, essential to the completion of the treaties, upon which the revival of the economic as well as the political life of the world depended. Whether Wilson might have salvaged more of his original program is a question still in doubt. On the whole, historical opinion has come to the conclusion that the settlement as agreed upon, had it actually been carried into effect, would have proved practicable and enduring.

The decision of Wilson to adjust to circumstances which he could not alter was made to appear in certain quarters as the bankruptcy of his entire program. The indictment against him was in part the expression of partisan prejudice; but it was chiefly inspired by disappointment. He had aroused hopes that his vision of Utopia could obliterate political facts. He now paid the price for the enthusiasm his program had evoked while it was still in the stage of generalities. His position would doubtless have been stronger had he not attempted to rationalize the compromises into such a form that they would fit into the design of his abstract principles. He thereby opened himself to the charge of hypocrisy and to the attack of perfectionists who joined with American isolationists in denunciation of the Versailles treaty.

But his prestige on the return to Washington in July of 1919 was still sufficient to assure ratification of the treaty and American participation in the League, assuming a reasonably sagacious political approach. At that time Senator Lodge himself, determined that the Republican party should not be split in two, hardly hoped for more than the reservations that would enable him to insist that he and his party had saved American independence from Wilsonian internationalism. But ratification depended upon conciliation of the Republican mild reservationists in such numbers as would compel Lodge to compromise.

The President could not bring himself to make the necessary concessions. His determination was hardened by the psychological effects of his illness and by his isolation from experienced political advisers. When it became clear that a two-thirds vote in the Senate could not be secured except upon the basis of the Lodge reservations, he would have been wise, without endorsing these reservations, to permit his followers to accept them and thus assure ratification. Historical opinion has tended toward the conclusion that since he had compromised in Paris he made a fatal mistake in refusing the compromises in Washington necessary to ratification. It was fatal, at least, in the sense that he thereby destroyed the crowning success of his policies, so nearly achieved, and his own immediate glorification. The action of the Senate, fortified, as it was made to appear, by the election of 1920, not merely kept the United States out of the League but apart from the close participation in European affairs upon which the Versailles treaty was predicated. The consequences of that withdrawal upon the authority of the League were momentous; no less so upon the relationships of the Great Powers with Germany and among themselves. In the debacle of the thirties, Europe and ultimately the United States paid a heavy price.

Woodrow Wilson completed his term as President in the shadow of political disaster. The endorsement of his program for which he called in the election of 1920 was refused him by an overwhelming vote. The dignity of his attitude in retirement and the pathos of his physical collapse assured him nationwide sympathy. But his dream of American leadership in world organization was dead and in a practical sense forgotten. Comfortably and blindly the United States fell back into the spirit of isolationism.

Abroad, the reputation of Wilson has never recovered from the reaction that followed the Peace Conference and the political disappearance of its leaders. His memory was summarily dismissed by conservative impatience at his attempt to inoculate Europe with his visionary principles and by liberal disappointment consequent upon his readiness to compromise them. Only in Geneva was adequate honor still paid him. The rise and fall of his hold on popular affection may be traced in the streets and squares that were named in tribute to his efforts on behalf of freedom, only to be renamed for some subsequent hero.

On this side of the Atlantic the upswing of opinion in Wilson's favor has been definite. But it has not yet become universal. He has suffered from the clash of contradictory elements in his temperament which affected not only his political career but the later judgment of history. It is by no means easy for the analytical historian to reach clear-cut conclusions in an estimate of Wilson in veiw of the fact that his political defects proceeded largely and often directly from his personal talents.

His outstanding characteristic as leader was an almost uncanny genius for persuasion, whether by the written or by the spoken word. In both respects Wilson greatly excelled. Through his peculiar and abiding influence upon individuals and upon small groups of high intelligence he exercised unheralded and permanent power in the nation. His outstanding capacity for persuading mankind in the large accounts in chief measure for the emphatic success of his legislative program on behalf of the New Freedom. But there was always the danger that by the very magic of his eloquence he would, like less distinguished evangelists in the religious field, bring his congregation into a process of conversion that was not to prove permanent. Thus he won the enthusiastic support of the people for the League as the chief buttress of American foreign policy; it was a revolutionary but a temporary achievement. Popular devotion to Wilson's great ideal turned out to be merely skin-deep and was soon lost in the other issues that beclouded the ill-fated election of 1920.

Another paradox in the public life of Wilson, when one comes to making up the main account, lies in the fact that his noblest attribute, an undeviating faith in principles, became a primary factor in the miscarriage of his plans for establishing them as a directive influence in the affairs of the world. No statesman has given to mankind a more cogent and elevated exposition of the infinite power and the enduring righteousness of justice and free-dom. But his illusion that such ideals could obliterate the stubborn facts of political life unsettled his policy at Paris and led directly to the disaster which he suffered at the hands of Senator Lodge.

Wilson's reputation has inevitably been heightened by the events of the quarter century that followed his death. The world received a terrible confirmation of his prophetic vision of the cataclysm which the League of Nations was designed to avert. The establish-ment of the United Nations consecrated the validity of his leader-ship, which had been mutilated at Paris and spurned by the United States Senate. Thus the defeat of 1920 became a sacrificial step toward his ultimate justification, and the failure of his League "a necessary part of the stumbling process," as Secretary Dulles puts it, "by which humanity develops the means for its own self-preservation."

But it would be a grievous error to permit the historical position of Wilson to depend upon the fortunes of any single institution no matter how impressive. It rests rather upon an invincible idea "so greatly conceived and set forth," as Edwin Alderman insisted immediately after Wilson's death, "that it must continue to grow into new and finer form and his fame must grow with it." Entirely apart from his contribution to a tangible instrument of political idealism, whether permanent or fugitive, Wilson is justified by faith. Magnificent in his leadership, he was too far in advance of his time. Men were not ready for the sacrifice of self-interest, the revolution in national outlook which his ideals demanded. But the inspiration of those ideals is permanent and no one has issued a more compelling call than Wilson's to devotion in their behalf, or more moving an example of undeviating faith in their nobility. Regardless of the ebb and flow of political and historical opinion, he stands forth as among the greatest of all prophets in the cause of international justice and freedom.

Long before entering active politics, in his address on "Leaders of Men," Wilson provided a clue to his own future claim to immortality. "Great reformers," he said, "do not, indeed, observe times and circumstances. Theirs is not a service of opportunity. They have no thought for occasion, no capacity for compromise. They are early vehicles of the Spirit of the Age. They are born of the very times that oppose them . . . theirs to hear the inarticulate voices that stir in the night-watches, apprising the lonely sentinel of what the day will bring forth."

ARTHUR S. LINK

✪

Wilson: Idealism and Realism

On March 4, 1913, a gaunt man walked to the stands outside the east front of the Capitol in Washington to take the oath of office as twenty-eighth President of the United States. Although his face was somber with a sense of high seriousness, it radiated strength and determination, and there was thrilling power in his voice as he summoned the American people to the tasks of national reconstruction. Eight years later, in 1921, he assisted in the rituals inaugurating his successor, Warren G. Harding. Now he was broken in body, and his drawn face reflected the pain that had come from his recent repudiation at the hands of the people during the election of 1920.

He was Woodrow Wilson, born in Staunton, Virginia, on December 28,* 1856, reared in Presbyterian manses in Georgia and the Carolinas, educated at Davidson College in North Carolina and Princeton University, trained in the study of law at the University of Virginia, and prepared for a career in teaching and scholarship at The Johns Hopkins University. He had taught successively from 1885 to 1902 at Bryn Mawr College in Pennsyl-

---

* Since the writing of this paper, it has been discovered that Wilson almost certainly was born at 12:45 A.M. on December 29, 1856 [ed.].

From Arthur S. Link, "The Higher Realism of Woodrow Wilson," *Journal of Presbyterian History*, XLI (March 1963), pp. 1–13; reprinted by permission of the *Journal of Presbyterian History*.

vania, Wesleyan University in Connecticut, and Princeton, and had served as president of the latter institution from 1902 to 1910. Plunging into the troubled sea of politics in 1910, he had won the Governorship of New Jersey and gone on with almost irresistible power to capture the Presidency in 1912. Then he had guided the destinies of the American people from 1913 to 1921 and helped to direct the destinies of the world during eight of the most critical years of the modern epoch.

I am happy to come before this particular audience in this venerable city to talk about the man who has been the subject of my main thought and work for twenty years. I must confess at the outset that I have prepared this paper with a definite purpose in mind. It is neither to praise Woodrow Wilson nor to bury him. The record of his contribution has its own integrity, and what little I could say would neither add to nor detract from it. It is not to bring you any new view of President Wilson, for I doubt that I could say anything really new about him at this point. My purpose is, rather, to attempt to pull together a number of thoughts and convictions that have been coursing through my mind during the past few years; in brief, to clarify my own conclusions about the subject of my life's work.

I have felt impelled to this undertaking in part by many conversations with English and German historians which have challenged my own emerging view of President Wilson. My experiences during a year abroad in 1958–1959 have brought home the fact that Europeans on the whole still view Wilson very much as many of them viewed him forty years ago at the end of the Paris Peace Conference and the great struggle in the United States over ratification of the Treaty of Versailles. This European image is, I think it is fair to say, one of a well-intentioned idealist, a man good by ordinary Christian standards, but essentially a destructive force in modern history because he was visionary, unrealistic, provincial, and ignorant of European problems; he was also zealous and messianic in conceit but devoid of either practical knowledge or the humility to follow others better informed than he. I do not think that this is an essentially unfair statement of the European point of view. It was, of course, the image of John Maynard Keynes, Georges Clemenceau, and most of the thoughtful European public at the end of the Peace Conference. It is the view still largely held by English, French, and German scholars alike if for different reasons.

I have felt impelled to my subject not only by recent forceful reminders of the strong survival of the old European image of President Wilson, but also by the emergence in our own country during the past few years of a new school of historical critics, and by their work in constructing an image of President Wilson that is remarkably like the older European one. Calling themselves realists, and drawing their inspiration from the distinguished diplomat-historian George Kennan, and the Austrian-trained authority in international relations Hans J. Morgenthau, now at the University of Chicago, these new American critics have found Wilson wanting because he did not think in terms of strategy, bases, and armed power, but dwelt too much in ethereal realms.

Are the old European and new American critics right, I have asked myself over and over during the past few years. Is this the image that I also see, the Wilson that I know? Were the Austrians right in thinking that his irresponsible preaching of a slogan, "self-determination," was primarily responsible for the destruction of the Hapsburg Empire? Were the Germans right in holding him responsible for what they regarded as the monstrous betrayal of Versailles? Were the French right in thinking that he prevented the imposition of the only kind of peace settlement upon Germany that could endure? Were the English and new American critics near the truth when they portrayed him as a tragic figure irrelevant in the modern world?

I must confess that I have sometimes been tempted to agree. No one who has ever given any serious attention to President Wilson's life could fail to agree that he was *primarily* a Christian idealist.

By this I mean a man who almost always tended to judge policies on a basis of whether they were right by Christian standards, not whether they brought immediate material or strategic advantage. I mean also a man whose foreign policies were motivated by the assumption that a nation as much as an individual should live according to the law of Christian love, and by a positive repudiation of the assumptions of the classical "realists" about international behavior.

No one who has given serious study to Wilson's career, moreover, could fail to agree that there is at least an appearance of reality about the old European and new American image. Wilson was not merely an idealist, but a crusading idealist. An orator of enormous eloquence and power, he was also a phrase-maker who more than once fell victim to the magic of his own words. In international relations he did not give undue weight to material forces or base his policies upon the assumption that nations must always act selfishly. At times he did seem to give the appearance of believing that he was a kind of messiah divinely appointed to deliver Europe from the cruel tyranny of history.

I have myself made all these criticisms and others more elaborately in my own writings. But they have never really satisfied me and do not satisfy me now. I do not think that they add up to an historical image that is accurate. Indeed, I cannot escape the conclusion that they altogether miss the main point and meaning of President Wilson's career.

The point, in my opinion, and the theme of this paper, is that among all the major statesmen and thoughtful critics of his age, President Wilson was in fact the supreme realist, and that because this is true, what he stood for and fought to accomplish has large meaning for our own generation.

This is, to be sure, a very broad, perhaps even an audacious, statement, one that does not mean very much unless we are careful to define our terms. A realist, I take it, is one who faces life and its situations without illusions; in short, one who can see realities or truth through the fog of delusion that normally shrouds the earth-bound individual. If the European and American critics of President Wilson who thought mainly in strategic and material terms, who measured national power by army divisions and naval bases, and the like, if *they* were realists, then President Wilson was a realist of a different sort. Sheerly for purposes of convenience, let us call his view of the national and international situations with which he had to cope a "higher realism," higher because more perceptive, more in accord with ultimate reality, more likely to win the long-run moral approval of societies professing allegiance to the common Western, humane, Christian traditions.

We still have not passed beyond the statement of a thesis and a definition of elementary terminology. There now remains the much more important task of seeing to what degree the evidence of Wilson's career supports my generalization. We obviously do not have time to review all the important events of Wilson's long and active career here. On the other hand, we cannot concentrate our attention on one aspect without running the risks of distortion. President Wilson actually had three separate public careers—as university president and educational statesman, as a domestic leader concerned almost exclusively with problems of political and economic reconstruction in the United States, and, finally, as a world statesman who attempted to give leadership in a movement for the reconstruction of the international community. He made large and seemingly different contributions in each field. And yet we must try to view his career and labors as a whole, for he was fundamentally the same man throughout. "His "higher realism" was no less a force in his leadership at home than abroad.

It was evident in a striking way in the first contributions that he made as a public leader, as president of Princeton University from 1902 to 1910. There were first the things that he did and tried to do for Princeton: his introduction of a systematic and meaningful course of undergradate study, and his positive repudiation of a conference, method of instruction to supplement the lecture system; and his proposal for the reorganization of undergraduate social life in order to elevate the intellectual climate of the university. By such plans and by his own inspiration, he not only transformed Princeton but also helped to transform higher education in the United States.

And yet Wilson made his greatest contributions in the field of education more by the things that he fought for than by what he did. For one thing, he stood for standards and academic integrity. For another, he had an exalted concept of the university and college and the role that they should play in preparing men and women for the nation's service because they were dedicated to the cause of truth and the intellectual enrichment of mankind. Finally, during an era of increasing specialization and degradation of undergraduate curricula by the introduction of all sorts of so-called useful programs of study, Wilson never ceased to remind fellow teachers and administrators that their first job was to help perpetuate the cultural traditions upon which Western civilization rested, not to teach students how to make money.

Who, we are entitled to ask, were the true "realists" in educational policy? Were they the alleged realists of Wilson's time, the sincere devotees of the new so-called progressive concepts and faddists, who were then beginning their long attack upon traditional studies and destroying the unity of university curricula? To ask the question is almost to answer it. The entire drive in American higher education during the past twenty years toward recovery of standards and unity in curricula and against the vulgarization that followed the widespread introduction of so-called useful courses of study—this entire movement, so full of promise, is testimony to the higher realism of Wilson's leadership in the academic world.

It was the same, I would suggest, with Wilson's leadership during his second career as Governor of New Jersey from 1911 to 1913 and President of the United States afterward. He came to political leadership at one of the most critical junctures in American history, at the high tide of what American historians call the progressive movement. For more than a quarter of a century the American people had been in revolt in city, state, and nation against corruption and venality among officeholders, irresponsibility on all levels of government, and, above all, the emergence and spread of great aggregations of economic power among railroads, banks, corporations, and so on, which were uncontrolled and often repudiated any responsibility to the people as a whole. This revolt was at the point of culmination at the very time that Wilson was catapulted into political life in 1910, and because this was true the American people were now confronted with certain choices that would determine their future political system and the role that government would hereafter play in making fundamental economic decisions.

There was, first, the choice concerning the reconstruction of the American political system. Some so-called realists of the time argued cogently from the facts that the very concept and structure of representative government were fatally defective, and that the answer lay either in direct democracy or in concentration of political power in fewer hands. "Realists" on the other side, eager to preserve a status quo that benefited their own economic interests, argued just as convincingly that the American constitutional system, with its diffusion and separation of powers, was the most nearly perfect form of government on earth.

There was, secondly, the choice concerning the role that government should play in economic life. At the one extreme were the "realists" who, talking in terms of immutable economic law, defended traditional American policies of *laissez faire* in an effort to protect their privileged position. At the other extreme were "realists" with a greater popular appeal—men who demanded a sweeping extension of the power of government to bridle all hitherto uncontrolled economic interests. Some of these were socialists, ready to abandon capitalism in the major sectors of the economy altogether. Others were progressives who believed in capitalism but argued that it had reached a permanent phase of semimonopolistic maturity in the United States and could be saved only by instituting sweeping and rigorous public controls over all important areas of national economic life.

It was Woodrow Wilson's privilege to play a decisive role in the determination of these choices. To the "realists" who had despaired of representative government in the cities and states he replied more by example than by precept—by giving a spectacular example of responsible leadership in action as Governor of New Jersey. By making representative government work on the local level he, along with a company of other leaders at the time, guaranteed its survival. To the "realists" (and he had earlier been among them) who had proclaimed the incapacity of the Presidential-Congressional system to cope with the great problems of national administration, Wilson responded, both by reasoned word and striking deed, by transforming that system and demonstrating that it had immensely greater capacities than the so-called realists had thought. He did this by transforming the office of President from that of an aloof presiding official into incomparably the most powerful force in the American constitutional system—the force that gave unity and direction not only to the other branches of the federal government but to public opinion as well. This, we can now see, was the "higher realism" of a man who well understood the weaknesses of the American institutional structure but who knew the fundamental strength of the American democracy far better than most so-called realists of his time.

I think that it is also fair to say that President Wilson demonstrated the same kind of long-run wisdom, or "higher realism," in leading the American people to adoption of new policies for the regulation of economic life. He rejected the arguments both of defenders of the status quo and of proponents of violent change as being unsound in principle and unacceptable to the majority of the people. And he (along with his supporters in Congress) instituted a series of measures to impose a large measure of public direction and control, but also to balance private initiative with public regulation in order to stimulate the enormous latent competitive energies of the people. In short, he laid the solid foundations of the present mixed American system of political economy, which, to the amazement and bafflement of many Europeans, works so curiously and so well. Viewing the subsequent development of the American economy within the framework erected by President Wilson and his colleagues, I think that we would have to conclude that Wilson's solution was the only "realistic" one that could have been adopted. It saved American capitalism by making it socially responsible and hence acceptable to the people, without, however, impeding the forces that are essential for growth in the capitalistic system.

I am sure that in talking about Wilson's "higher realism" in meeting domestic challenges, I have simply been saying things and making judgments with which virtually every historian of the United States would readily agree. It is precisely this "higher realism" that has entitled Wilson to rank, by the agreement of American historians, among the four or five successful Presidents in our history. In talking about Wilson's policies and contributions in the realm of foreign affairs, I am, I know, on more controversial ground. Wilson was magnificently prepared for leadership in internal affairs by long study of American history and institutions. He had little if any preparation for leadership in the world at large; indeed, at the outset of his tenure in the White House he had no serious interest in foreign affairs. At the outset and later he made mistakes that still seriously impair his record. Even so, I cannot but conclude that President Wilson on the whole showed the same kind of wisdom and long-range vision and understanding, in short, "higher realism," in his third career as international statesman as he had already revealed in his first two careers at home.

This, I know, is a big statement, and I would like to preface it with a few generalizations about Wilson's thought and character as a diplomat in order to lay foundations for some later observations.

The first is the most obvious and the one with which most

historians would agree, namely, that President Wilson was, as I have already said, above all an idealist in the conduct of foreign affairs, one who subordinated immediate goals and material interests to what he considered to be superior ethical standards and moral purposes. His idealism was perhaps best revealed in his thinking about the purposes that the United States should serve in the world. The mission of America, he said over and over and sincerely believed, was not a mission of aggrandizement of material power but one of service to mankind. It was a mission of peace, of sacrifice, of leading the nations into a new international community organized to achieve right ends.

Secondly, all of Wilson's thinking about international relations was conditioned, in general, by a loathing for war and, in particular, by a conviction that physical force should never be used to achieve selfish and material aims.

Thirdly, Wilson was actually in many ways "realistic," even by conventional standards, in his thinking about the methods in the conduct of foreign relations. For example, he used armed force in the classic way to achieve certain diplomatic objectives in Mexico and the Caribbean. He understood the meaning of the term "balance of power." He was keenly aware of the relevance of material interests and had few illusions about the fundamental bases of international behavior. It is, one must say, the sheerest nonsense to talk about him as an impractical idealist and visionary.

Fourthly, while admitting that there were times when a nation had no recourse but to use armed force in international disputes, and while using force himself on behalf of the American government on certain occasions, President Wilson never permitted war's neuroses and fascinations either to derange his reason or to obscure the political objectives for which force was being used. Hence he was never the victim of that greatest twentieth-century delusion, that it is necessary to win wars even at the risk of losing everything for which wars are fought.

This is a very imperfect characterization of the thought and character of Wilson the diplomatist, but it may help us to understand his policies during the greatest tragedy of the modern epoch and the event that raised the gravest challenges to his leadership—the First World War. It was for Wilson a period with three distinct stages—the period of American neutrality, from August, 1914 to April 1917; the period of American belligerency, from April, 1917 to November, 1918; and the period of peace-making, from November, 1918 to June, 1919. The challenges of each period were different, but he met them all, on the whole, with the same "higher realism" that had characterized his leadership at home.

His policies during the first period can best be briefly described by saying that from the outbreak of the war in Europe to the beginning of the German unlimited submarine campaign in early 1917, President Wilson tried as hard as any man could have done to be neutral, to make the necessary accommodations to the exercise of belligerent power, and to engage in stern defense of American rights only when they could not, because fundamental human principles were involved, be compromised.

Some of the recent American "realists" have joined the older English and French critics in charging Wilson with impractical idealism precisely because he did follow such a course—because he did not rally the American people to preparation for what they have said was an inevitable participation; because he conducted long and patient negotiations to avoid a break with Germany; because he did not undertake large and early measures of assistance to the Allies and thus help to shorten the duration of Europe's agony; because he refused throughout the period of American neutrality even to align the American people and their government morally on the Allied side.

Looking back upon the final outcome, as we are entitled to do, we well might wonder who the true realists were during this period. So-called "realists," or President Wilson, who in an almost uncanny way kept himself immune from the emotional hysterias and passions that seized other men; who believed that the causes of the

war were so complex and remote that it was impossible to assess
the blame; who, overborne by the tragedy of the event, fought
desperately to preserve American neutrality so that he could perform the healing task of reconciliation once the nations of Europe
had come to some sense; who believed that an enduring peace
could come only through a "peace without victory," a "peace
between equals"? Who were the deluded men who had lost sight of
reality? The European leaders who thought that they could win
decisive victories on the battlefields and on or under the seas, and
who thought that they could impose their nations' wills upon other
great peoples? Or Wilson, who thought that they were momentarily
mad?

The climactic confrontation, the supreme reckoning between so-
called realists and the alleged impractical idealist, came once the
United States had been forced into the conflict and Germany was
defeated. It did not occur earlier, because the British and French
leaders had refused to permit it to occur before the Armistice was
safely signed. But it could not then be long postponed, for the
Allied leaders had matured their plans, and President Wilson had
meanwhile formed a peace program of his own and announced it
to the world in the Fourteen Points address and other speeches.

There is no need to review the turbulent events of the Paris
Peace Conference here. They are familiar enough, to begin with;
but a detailed account of them now would obscure my larger
purpose—to look back upon the Paris settlement and, while
looking back, to attempt to see who the true realists were.

The supreme task of the victors at Paris in 1919 was, obviously,
to work out a peace settlement and reconstruct an international
order that could endure. It had to be a peace that could survive the
ebbing of passions and hatreds that consumed Europe in 1919. It
had to be a peace that could survive because it could command the
approval of the German people. Above all, it had to be the kind of
settlement that would endure because it could retain the long-run
support of the American and English peoples, even of the French

people. The necessity of constructing this kind of settlement was, as we can now see clearly, the supreme reality of peace-making in 1919. We must, therefore, judge men and measures at the Paris Conference according to whether they met this test or not.

By this criterion I do not see how any fair historian can but conclude that the so-called realists at Paris—the dedicated if cynical Clemenceau, concerned only about the destruction of the ancient foe and the future security of France; the well-intentioned Lloyd George, who had given so many hostages to war passions at home and to the Commonwealths that he was no longer a free man; and the Italians, Sonnino and Orlando, eager only for spoils—how could they be called anything other than sublime irrationalists and dreamers? Theirs was a dream, a nightmare, of unreality. Given the task of reconstructing Europe and preventing a future war, they would have responded by attempting to perpetuate the division of Europe and by making a new war almost inevitable.

On the other side and standing usually in solitary if splendid isolation was the alleged impractical idealist fighting for the only kind of a settlement that had any chance of survival—for a peace of reconciliation, for disarmament by victors as well as vanquished, against annexations and indemnities, and for a new international organization that would include former enemy states as active members from the beginning. Over and over he warned that this was the only kind of peace that would prove acceptable to the American people in the short run and to the moral opinion of the world in the long run, in short, the only kind of settlement that could endure. It should require little reference to events that followed the Paris Conference to demonstrate the "higher realism" of President Wilson's views.

If proof is needed on specific points, one could cite, for example, Wilson's point of view on the problem of reparations. Over and over he insisted, and with a steadfast consistency, that reparations should be compensation for specific willful damage only, not indemnity; that the Germans should not be saddled with a debt that was heavier than they could carry; and that there should be a time limit to the obligation that the German nation should be forced to assume. What the Allied leaders demanded and finally obtained is well-known to any student of modern history. What the realistic solution of this problem was is now too obvious for comment. Or, as a second example, one might cite Wilson's attitude toward the Russian Revolution—how he saw the deeply rooted causes of that cataclysm and the futility of any Western effort to suppress it by military force; and how the realism of his attitude contrasted to the egregious folly of so-called realists who thought that it lay within their power to change the course of Russian history.

The result of the clash between European so-called realism and Wilsonian so-called idealism was of course the Treaty of Versailles, that compromise that violated the terms of the agreement by which the Germans had stopped fighting, and made a mockery of some of the principal planks in the American President's peace program. Why, it is fair to ask, did President Wilson permit such a peace to be made and sign the treaty embodying it? The answer, I submit, is that it was "higher realism" that drove him to this difficult decision. Having won many of the things for which he had been fighting, at least partially, he had to give as well as to take, for he could not impose his will entirely upon his colleagues. He signed the Versailles treaty in the conviction that the passage of time and the treaty's new creation, the League of Nations, would almost certainly operate to rectify what he knew were the grievous mistakes of the Peace Conference. He signed the Versailles treaty, in short, because he believed that it was the best settlement possible in the circumstances of 1919.

What President Wilson hoped would occur did of course in large part take place during the 1920's and early 1930's, even though alleged realists in the United States combined with authentic visionaries to repudiate Wilson's work and prevent their government from playing the role of mediating leadership within the League of Nations of which Wilson had dreamed. The great tragedy of the postwar period was not that the Versailles treaty was imperfect. It was that the forces of reconciliation could not operate rapidly enough without American leadership in the League, that France and Great Britain had neither the will nor the strength to defend the treaty alone during the 1930's and, above all, that the German people submitted to demonic forces that promised a speedy rectification of all the injustices of Versailles. But this is precisely what President Wilson, in another flash of "higher realism," predicted would occur if the so-called realists, both in the United States and in Europe, continued to have their way.

That is the age-old question, whether the so-called realists or the higher realists shall have their way in determination of national and international policies. President Wilson survives a more powerful force in history than when he lived because he gave us the supreme demonstration in the twentieth century of higher realism in statesmanship.

This, obviously, was no accident. Woodrow Wilson's "higher realism" was the product of insight and wisdom informed by active Christian faith. He was not, fundamentally, a moralist, as he so often seemed to be, but a man who lived in faith, trying to be guided by the Holy Spirit in meeting the complex problems of a changing nation and world. Using one of his own metaphors we can say that the light of heaven gleamed upon his sword. His precepts and ideals will be relevant so long as democracy endures, so long as men seek after a new international community organized for peace and the advancement of mankind.

✪

Building on the Wilsonian Heritage

It is a mark of the great man that there are many roads to his understanding. I myself came to know Wilson by way of an interest in American politics and American history. But despite this I have never felt as close to Wilson in the country of his birth and of his Presidency, as I do in Geneva. One reason, of course, is too obvious to require stating; it takes visible form in that Palais des Nations which must always be his greatest visible memorial. But Wilson's links with Geneva are not confined to the Geneva of the League. Long before he had begun to clothe his ideals of international order in institutional form, an earlier Geneva, the Geneva of John Calvin, had been at work on him shaping those ideals themselves.

Many biographers of Wilson have stressed the Calvinist element in his inheritance. He was not only the son of a Presbyterian minister; he also came, on his mother's side, of a long line of Presbyterian divines stretching back ultimately to his family's beginning in the intensely Calvinist society of seventeenth-century Scotland and Ulster. It can hardly be doubted that Wilson's ideals of law and order, his exacting concept of duty (for men and nations alike), his conviction of America's high and precious

From Herbert G. Nicholas, "Wilsonianism at Mid-Century," *Centenaire Woodrow Wilson* (Geneva, 1956), pp. 95–110; reprinted by permission of the author.

destiny to lead the world into the paths of peace—all this can be traced back to the teaching of the *Institutes* and to the theocracy of the sixteenth-century Geneva city-state. To the first generation of Wilson's critics—a postwar generation which had largely rejected all theological forms of thinking, Calvinist or other—Wilson's Calvinism was a convenient target for cynical disparagement. To this were ascribed the elements of hypocrisy, self-deception and utopianism which disillusioned idealists, in particular, detected in his character. Seldom did these critics observe that there was another sage who had presided at Woodrow Wilson's nativity besides John Calvin. Their failure to notice him was the more surprising since he had presided, for most of them, at their own spiritual nativities also. He too was a citizen of Geneva—though a more disreputable one. I refer, of course, to Jean Jacques Rousseau.

It is doubtful whether Wilson would himself have claimed Rousseau as a spiritual godparent. There is little explicit Rousseauism in his speeches or writings. But as the chosen leader of the Democratic party and as the apostle of the "New Freedom," Wilson regarded himself as in many ways the twentieth-century standard-bearer of Jeffersonianism. And just as Presbyterianism was the New World application of the principles of Calvin, so was Jeffersonianism the American version of the gospel of *The Social Contract*. In Wilson's utterances the first may have been more explicit, but in his thinking, particularly in those unquestioned premises which lay almost unconsciously at the basis of his thought, the second was often dominant. When the two creeds clashed, it was often the Calvinist in him that gave way. Thus the belief in original sin is replaced by an illusion of human perfectibility; the Calvinist realism about the role of power in the ordering of human societies is supplanted by a Rousseauesque reliance upon the operations of the general will; the highly qualified and circumscribed democracy of Calvin's Geneva becomes the open and universal Utopia of *The Social Contract*. No one will under-

stand Wilson who does not appreciate these two strands in his
make-up. Most of those incisive and compelling depictions of his
personality drawn by the survivors of Versailles have achieved
their effect by a convenient neglect of whichever component might
complicate the impression the writer most wanted to convey. But a
fair assessment of the strength and weaknesses of the Wilsonian
Weltanschauung can only be arrived at if proper regard is paid to
the dual sources of his philosophy.

What was his philosophy? In what did Wilsonianism consist?
One may answer this question, as many critics have done, by
looking at the results of Wilson's labors—the Covenant, the
Treaty, etc.—and then, arguing back from their merits or demerits,
demonstrate the faults or virtues of their creator. But such a
method is by no means satisfactory. To do this is to ignore the
obvious fact that Wilson was not alone as a creator; his creations
bear the marks of other hands as well. We cannot point to any
institution or settlement and say "There you can see the pure
embodiment of Wilsonianism." There is always an alloy of French
or British—or even of un-Wilsonian American—concepts in the
international structure he did so much to build. Most politicians
with theories to translate into practice realize in advance that
something of this sort is bound to occur. Accordingly even the
formulation of their theories, the orientation of their dreams, take
into account beforehand something of the concessions that will
have to be made at the conference table. But Wilson was not of
this type. His philosophy was formulated three thousand miles
away from the continent on which it was mainly to be implemented. It embodied the minimum of advance concessions to alien
views. It was perhaps, therefore, particularly liable to buckle under
the pressure of discrepant reality. But if its true nature is to be
appreciated, it is all the more necessary, in consequence, to look at
it in itself. The "Wilsonianism" of my title is therefore to be
understood as referring to the ideals of the President rather than to
the practice of the leader of the American delegation, at times

indeed to Wilson the professor rather than to Wilson the diplomatist.

How then does this "Wilsonianism" appear in 1956, more than a generation later, through the perspective of yet another world war and yet another "League to Enforce Peace"? One element in it has certainly receded from the forefront of public consciousness—at least in Europe, though rather less so in the U.S.A. That is the concept of an international order based upon what Wilson variously called "the reign of law" or "respect of the common law of civilized society." We have seen so much international lawbreaking in our time (however "law" in this context may be defined) that we have become first cynical and then, I think more wisely, skeptical. Skeptical, that is, about the possibility of enacting (and still more of enforcing) a code of international law in advance of the establishment of a world community whose natural expression it would be.

But to ascribe to Wilson a belief in a code of law and an international law-enforcing agency is in fact to misrepresent his thinking. Although on this, as on many other points of his international credo, Wilson's thought lacked precision, the language he used gives a fair clue to his meaning. He talks of a "common law"—by analogy, obviously, to that Common Law of his British inheritance which was entirely uncodified, which was built up piecemeal by judges working on the precedents of their predecessors, and whose acceptance by Parliament and the law enforcing agencies was a consequence of its conformity to the prevailing standards of justice and morality. Similarly Wilson talks of a "definite tribunal of opinion" as his enforcing agency, not of an armed police force which acts against the lawbreakers and brings them to justice. No doubt such a conception has perils of its own, as witness the exchange in the commission that drafted the Covenant, when Larnaude asked, who or what body would pass upon the question "Is a treaty inconsistent with the Covenant?" Would it be the Council or a special tribunal? Wilson answered promptly

"The decision will lie with the court of public opinion," upon which Larnaude turned to Bourgeois to inquire: "Tell me, mon ami, am I at the Peace Conference or in a madhouse?"

But in fact does not the whole of our experience since Versailles confirm the absolute rightness of Wilson's reply? We have not advanced to a stage of international organization when world courts can usefully hand down decisions on matters which great powers regard as crucial for their security or interest. We are still at the stage when the function of international tribunals, in all spheres save a few technical or semitechnical ones in which states have made voluntary relinquishments of sovereignty, is a strictly limited one. It is not, as in an established national community, to act as the instruments of the public will, but rather to act almost as the exact opposite—to gather together, to focus what little public will there is in the hope that the intrinsic justice of their decisions (rather than any reverence accorded to their status or their procedures) will win them an enhanced respect from the public opinion of mankind. This is a slow, erratic—two steps forward, one step back—and often undignified process. But Wilson was surely right in thinking that it was the only possible one.

The natural corollary of this Wilsonian conception was of course the emphasis on mutual guarantees which found expression in Article X of the Covenant—what Wilson described as its "backbone," the article without which the League "would hardly be more than an influential debating society." Through this article "the common law of civilized society" is to take action against those who "invade the right." At an early stage in the argument over Wilson's policies it was pointed out how much mutual guarantees of the status quo, as of any status quo, were incompatible with a strict application of the principle of self-determination. The validity of such criticisms is too obvious and their melancholy exemplification in the history of the interwar years is too familiar for me to recapitulate them. What was less quickly realized was the hollowness of the collective security concept itself.

We know now that you cannot establish security merely by every-one promising to combine with everyone else to suppress an aggressor. Joint action in wartime presupposes joint planning in time of peace. Either the intending aggressor is a member of the collectivity whose security is to be guaranteed or he is not. If he is, previous joint planning is impossible; if he is not, then the international collectivity is less than universal. Both the League and the United Nations have been less than universal; to the extent that they have been so their claim to represent the moral opinion of mankind is impaired—a fact which Wilson clearly recognized; hence his own desire for universality. Unfortunately the most successful recorded instance of collective action in defense of territorial integrity—the Korean war—was undertaken against a nonmember nation and was initiated at a moment when its most active accomplice among the member nations, the U.S.S.R., was foregoing its membership rights in a fit of sulks. We hail—and rightly hail—the U.N. action in Korea as a great forward step in the establishment of an international order. Yet in one third of the world it was regarded as an imperialist maneuver and, even if the falsity of Communist propaganda could be totally exposed, would still be regarded as such by most Chinese and many Asiatics so long as present-day China was not a member of the United Nations. An aggressor will never grant moral endorsement to the use of power against himself. More important, fellow travelers with aggression (without whom no successful aggression has ever yet taken place) will not grant it either, if they feel themselves excluded from the community whose power is being employed. Yet their exclusion, at least in part, is a prime essential of successful concerted action for the organization of peace. Hence the paradox that in the world of sovereign states the actions even of the lawful are liable to lose their moral validity in the eyes of the law-breakers; only the wholly impotent are wholly virtuous.

This was a paradox which Wilson found hard to accept. Two weaknesses in his philosophy hampered him here. The first was his illusion of American innocence. Because the United States lay outside the most evident manifestations of the European power system—secret alliances, boundary manipulations, etc.—Wilson conceived his country to be entirely disinterested in her attitude toward world settlements. They would be, he told his collaborators on the *George Washington,* as they sailed toward Paris, "the only disinterested people at the Peace Conference." America, to him, was distinguished from the rest of the world by being uninvolved in all previous history, by being in a condition that only Rousseau would have thought possible (Calvin would certainly have known better) of original virtue. With the "causes" and "objects" of the war she entered in 1917 she had, said Wilson, no concern. "We have nothing material of any kind to ask for ourselves, and are quite aware that we are in no sense or degree parties to the present quarrel." There was enough truth in this to get it—for a short time and in the United States—believed. But as the Senate was soon to teach the President, and as Mr. Walter Lippmann and others had subsequently to demonstrate to latter-day Senators, there *were* American interests that had to be safeguarded, there *were* links between American security and the European power system which could be ignored only at the peril both of Europe and of the United States.

The Wilsonian illusion of American innocence was also extended to the system of government which America had adopted. Democracies, in Wilson's view, were the only really peace-loving countries. "Only free people," he said, "could hold their purpose and their honor steady to a common end and prefer the interests of mankind to any narrow interest of their own." Not only is the world to be made safe *for* democracy; it is to be made safe *by* democracy. Idealist disappointment with the first democratic peace settlement has provoked far too sweeping a rejection of the Wilsonian thesis here. Whatever may be said by sentimental addicts of the Old Diplomacy about the superior tractability of autocratic governments at the conference table, there can be no doubt at all that in the twentieth-century world, democracies are, by and large, naturally pacific and mutually compatible in a way that dictatorships, personal or collective, are not. The history of the thirties is a decisive proof of this. For those who lived through them, argument can add nothing to experience. But for those who were already too old to realize what was happening, and those now too young to remember it, the Wilsonian demonstration can still be recommended.

Unfortunately, however, Wilson pushed it too far. He ignored the element of self-interest that persists in the calculations and conduct of even the most democratic of democracies; above all he never allowed for the particular virulence of a democracy run amok. *Corruptio optimi pessima.* Had Wilson lived to see Nazi Germany overrun Europe, he would have seen how it was the democratic elements in Naziism that gave to its lust for conquest its peculiarly fanatical and intractable force. His conviction that all error resided in governments and that the people were always and everywhere virtuous led him into some of the gravest follies of the Paris Peace Conference. Even more unfortunately, his sentimental illusion persisted after him to bedevil much of the interwar thinking about the role and prospects of the League of Nations. It provided a moralistic prop for the policies of appeasement in Europe and isolationism in the U.S.A. In the postwar years, it stimulated wishful thinking about the nature of the Soviet regime and the significance of the Chinese revolution.

This illusion of popular virtue, of course, was only a manifestation of a more deep-seated characteristic of Wilsonian internationalism, its evasion of the problem of power. Wilson the warmaker had no aversion to the use of force. "Force, Force to the utmost, Force without stint or limit." But once the war is won, what then? What is the place of force in what one might call the normal relations of nations? To this question Wilson had no considered answer. The whole bent of this thinking was toward regarding the League not as a way of organizing or taming power, but as a substitute for power. He "identified collective security," as Mr. Lippmann says, "with antipathy to alliances," rather than "with the constructive development of alliances." In the League, the world had a parliament; what then did it want with a police force? Even in relation to the American people, whose psychology Wilson usually well understood, this way of envisaging the League was probably a mistake. It is possible that if Wilson had presented the League to them as an instrument for preserving their security (rather than as a kind of New Jerusalem), they would have responded even in 1920 by accepting membership in some form or another.

This way of treating the League as a substitute for power led directly to the erroneous thinking of the interwar years about disarmament, the thinking that sought disarmament as an end in itself, that divorced it from the establishment of a system of security, that in its most extravagant form, as sometimes in Britain and the United States, even regarded the private manufacture of armaments as the basic cause of war. To blame all this on Wilson would be less than fair, but the statesman who originally wanted a clause in Article VIII of the Covenant empowering the League Council "to inquire into the possibility of abolishing compulsory military service" and who at the same time took the lead in resisting French demands for establishing international control of armaments certainly stimulated some of the comfortable illusions that rendered the League impotent in its moments of peril.

We are in little danger today of falling into Wilson's mistake of neglecting power. The painful experiences of our time have made us proof against this particular error. We may even have gone too far in the other direction and, like some of the apostles of the new *Realpolitik* in the study of international relations, have allowed ourselves to be mesmerized by the phenomenon of power. (Perhaps indeed I should use an even less flattering metaphor and describe this state of mind as a kind of masochistic self-immolation.) We may have become too skeptical about the possibility and desirability of outlawing certain uses and forms of power—the hydrogen bomb for instance—or about the value of disarmament per se. In our proper concern to see justice clothed in power we may even have developed a kind of prudery about justice in the nude. Idealism naked can cause the same kind of embarrassment in twentieth-century politics as sex once provoked in nineteenth-century society. Nevertheless, I think we are today in a healthier, because more balanced, moral posture than the one which Wilson would have had us assume. We have retained what was most valid in his concept of a world organization that would mobilize opinion for peace and for international order; at the same time we have allowed for the realities of power in interstate relations and for the demands of like-minded nations that they should combine for common defense. The regional security organizations which have grown up inside the U.N. supply something which the League lacked. I would like to think that the President who returned to Paris with a demand that Article X be revised to provide for the explicit recognition of the Monroe Doctrine would not find in NATO and SEATO anything unduly shocking. But I am afraid I should be hard put to it to find an explicit recognition anywhere in Wilson's recorded utterances that such "balance of power alliances" (as, outside the American continent, he always described them) were in fact consonant with the League ideal. We have, I think, progressed to a new realism here.

We have also, of course, filled in another gap in Wilson's thinking about power in international relations. We now recognize—on the whole pretty adequately (at least where our own interests are not involved)—the reality and pervasiveness of economic power. We are all Keynesians now. In a sense that even Etienne Mantoux would not have disputed, *The Economic Consequences of the Peace* have taught us their lesson. There is nothing like losing your economic power for making you conscious of the reality of it. The poor are greater realists than the rich. And Europe since Wilson has become such a poor mendicant that it not only has a new consciousness of the power of riches but, by the importunity of its begging, has made America conscious of it as well. In this connection the whole contrast between Wilson's world and ours is summed up in the fact that whereas in his day "dollar diplomacy" was a naughty word, today it is a pillar of the free world.

Not that Wilson's thinking about international economics was by any means wholly wrong. After all, the prophet of the New Freedom knew something about the relation between economics and politics even if it was primarily in an American context. There is nothing wrong with the third of the Fourteen Points as a statement of what is economically and, ultimately politically, desirable. "The removal of all economic barriers and the establishment of an equality of trade conditions" are still valid objectives both in themselves and as a means to international appeasement. The trouble is that they require as much positive organizing and underpinning as the structure of political security itself. Agitation for a mere removal of tariffs, quotas and the like will get nowhere by itself in a world in which economic power is so unevenly distributed and in which nations persist, reasonably or unreasonably, in subordinating Economic man to Cultural man, Social Security man, or, quite simply, National man.

"National man." He is the figure that rises dominant from the mists of Versailles. If we are to believe such observers as Robert Lansing, he is the genie that escaped from the bottle when Wilson took the cork out, in the sacred name of self-determination. In fact, of course, he was at large already, disrupting the Hapsburg Empire from within, organizing revolutions all over Europe, sometimes adopting strange Marxist disguises but essentially the same everywhere in his intractable, explosive, self-determining energy. Wilson did not release him, much less invent him. He simply recognized and understood him. And on this, to my own way of thinking, rests Wilson's most enduring claims to remembrance. Wilson, at the same time as he asserted the claims of internationalism, also emphasized the imperatives of nationalism. For this, he has often been blamed—and understandably so when one views the harm wreaked in Europe and elsewhere by nationalism gone berserk. The blame, however, is misapplied, for just as the nationalisms recognized at Versailles were in existence long before the treaty, so the stream of nationalist movements which has persisted from Wilson's day to ours owes little if anything to his encouragement. Surely, if there are any "inevitable" trends in history, this is one of them. No man or government can fairly be saddled with the responsibility for it. In the thirties it was morally comforting to think that nationalism was a kind of disease of effete Western societies, a virus injected into the bloodstream by fanatical dictators. Whatever support such a view might have won for itself in the second decade of the twenty-year armistice was speedily destroyed in the ensuing war itself. It was then demonstrated over and over again that it was nationalist feeling that sustained Britain's morale in the bleak days of 1940, that rallied Russia under the onslaught of 1941 and 1942, and that inspired resistance movements all over Europe from the Atlantic to the Aegean. Since the war, nationalism has burned like a prairie fire across Asia and is obviously about to do the same in Africa. In the face of manifestations as intense and as scattered as Cyprus, Burma, Korea, Morocco, Argentina, who can dare to say that "self-determination" is an outdated ideal, that nationalism is out of place in the modern world? At times it almost seems as if it *is* the modern world!

In recognizing this fact, in accepting the right of self-determination as something which people can only be denied if you are going to deny them all other human rights as well, Wilson was surely being the supreme realist. By comparison imperial apologists, economic integrators, World Federalists were all alike, if in varying degrees, fantasy-mongers. On this, his various critics have been refuted, not by logic, which indeed was often on their side, but by history, which was on his. It was reasonable to point out, as

E. H. Carr does, that Wilson confused the subjective right of self-determination with the objective fact of nationality, that he assumed that "states" and "nations" would coincide, "that states should be constituted on a national basis and that nations ought to form states." Without doubt Wilson was guilty of this confusion, but as Mr. Carr himself points out, "in Western Europe and in most of those overseas countries whose civilization was derived from Western Europe, the distinction had ceased to have practical importance." Elsewhere, of course, the lack of objective criteria of nationhood has enormously increased the difficulties of applying the principle of self-determination—notably in the East where it has come into conflict with differences of race, religion and political sophistication. The difficulty of applying it is, however, one thing; the insistent demand for it remains. In face of this demand it is simply no use deploring it, or suggesting alternatives. All our experience with Asian and Asiatic nationalism since Wilson's time simply confirms the rightness of his conviction that there is no alternative to conceding it.

This is true even where, as often in the Versailles settlement, the political entities so created are economically unsatisfactory. Without doubt we are moving into an age of larger and larger economic units, but it does not follow that political boundaries should be dictated by economic planners. The globe is the only completely viable economic unit; short of that, people can have only as large an economy as they are prepared to pay for, and all the evidence suggests that when this price involves the surrender of national identity most peoples are reluctant to pay it. Here too Wilson was right; there is nothing in our experience to suggest that peoples can be coaxed out of their desire to be themselves by assurances that they will be better off economically if they remain or become part of somebody else. The slow progress of European Union, the separation of India and Pakistan, the one-hundred-fifty-year-old refusal of Canada to become a forty-ninth state—in this matter the experience of the Old, Very Old, and New Worlds all points the same moral.

The same intractability of nationalism has made it proof against the apocalyptic threats of the One-Worlders. Logic is on their side. Every hydrogen bomb explosion is a dress rehearsal in miniature of the doom with which they threaten us. But so far at least there is no sign that men can be frightened out of their national loyalties any more than they can be bought out of them. Wilson knew nothing of hydrogen or atom bombs, but the emotional impact of Paschendaele and Verdun was not sensibly less on his generation than Hiroshima and Nagasaki were on ours, and he knew better than to suppose, in his most utopian moments, that even Europeans would be willing to erect a supergovernment on the ruins of the Old Diplomacy. Were Wilson alive today he would not, I submit, be numbered among the ranks of the World Federalists. Here again Wilson was essentially the realist. He did not want world government and, more important, he knew that his own and other countries did not want it either. What he wanted was voluntary cooperation. At moments—his cloudier moments—he may have used language as misleadingly utopian as Rousseau's, in which the League or the Covenant took on the more mystical, panacealike aspects of the *Volonté Générale*. The diffusion of such woolly thinking, after Wilson's death, undoubtedly played a major part in the enfeeblement of the League itself. But in building the League, Wilson was proceeding as an eminently practical statesman, constructing a form of association which would promote the maximum international cooperation and at the same time respect all legitimate national aspirations. The failure of the League—if failure it was—was not ascribable to inherent weaknesses in its conception or structure. It was ascribable to the intrinsic difficulties of the task it had to face—the fusing of national wills into an international purpose. To do this required time, patience and repeated endeavor. That the first attempt should not have succeeded is no matter for surprise nor a discredit to its inceptor. There is no short-cut to the international society, not even any beaten track.

To those of us who have survived the breakdown of Wilson's League, there has been given the opportunity to build another in its place. We have been able to profit from his mistakes, and, we like to think, the new structure is in consequence going to prove more lasting than the old. But if so, the essential soundness of his conception is only the more confirmed, because the U.N., for all its differences, rests basically upon the same principles and methods as its predecessor. It accepts, as Wilson did, the face of nationalism and the need for internationalism. We are more skeptical than he was about the natural harmony of national wills. We feel more at home with the Calvinist elements of his thinking than with such optimistic strains as he caught from the *Vicaire Savoyard*. But that ought not to lead us into pessimism, still less into an utter intolerance of those new nationalisms which, intoxicated with the experience of determining themselves, prove rough neighbors for older states who have been longer used to the ways of freedom. In earlier days the text "Compel them to come in" was used to give scriptural warrant for intolerance; in our own day there is a certain risk that "Compel them to keep out" might be used to serve a comparable purpose. But now less even than in Wilson's day would such a policy prove justifiable in international affairs. Now that we have to some extent devolved the security functions of the U.N. onto other organs we can the more completely realize his own conception of the League as a tribunal of world opinion, an agency devoted to the maximization of agreement by the processes of free discussion and, wherever possible, free cooperation. Whether that is what Wilson, if he were among us in 1956, would himself advocate, we cannot, of course, know. But to me it seems a purpose wholly consonant with the ideals of the apostle of self-determination and of the prophet of internationalism.

Selected Bibliography

The basic published documentary resource for a study of Woodrow Wilson and his time is *The Papers of Woodrow Wilson* (Princeton, N.J., 1966–   ), being edited by Arthur S. Link and his associates. Four of the projected forty volumes of this series will have been published by the spring of 1968. Ray Stannard Baker and William E. Dodd (eds.), *The Public Papers of Woodrow Wilson* (6 vols., New York, 1925–1927); E. David Cronon (ed.), *The Political Thought of Woodrow Wilson* (Indianapolis, 1965); John Wells Davidson (ed.), *A Crossroads of Freedom, the 1912 Campaign Speeches of Woodrow Wilson* (New Haven, Conn., 1956); August Heckscher (ed.), *The Politics of Woodrow Wilson* (New York, 1956); David W. Hirst (ed.), *Woodrow Wilson: Reform Governor* (Princeton, N.J., 1965); and T. H. Vail Motter (ed.), *Leaders of Men, by Woodrow Wilson* (Princeton, N.J., 1952), are useful sources for Wilson's most important incidental writings and speeches. Wilson's two major books, *Congressional Government* and *Constitutional Government in the United States,* are available in paperback.

The three major biographies are Ray Stannard Baker, *Woodrow Wilson: Life and Letters* (8 vols., Garden City, N.Y., 1927–1939); Arthur S. Link, *Wilson* (5 vols., Princeton, N.J., 1947–1965); and Arthur Walworth, *Woodrow Wilson* (2 vols., New York, 1958). Henry W. Bragdon, *Woodrow Wilson: The Academic Years* (Cambridge, Mass., 1967), deals most extensively with Wilson's early life, while James Kerney, *The Political Education of Woodrow Wilson* (New York, 1926), is a shrewd study of Wilson's entry into politics. There are numerous brief biographies. The best are Herbert C. F.

Bell, *Woodrow Wilson and the People* (New York, 1945); John M. Blum, *Woodrow Wilson and the Politics of Morality* (Boston, 1956); John A. Garraty, *Woodrow Wilson* (New York, 1956); and Arthur S. Link, *Woodrow Wilson, A Brief Biography* (Cleveland and New York, 1963).

The Wilson circle did not produce many distinguished memoirs. The three that reveal most about Wilson the man are Cary T. Grayson, *Woodrow Wilson: An Intimate Memoir* (New York, 1960); Herbert Hoover, *The Ordeal of Woodrow Wilson* (New York, 1958); and Joseph P. Tumulty, *Woodrow Wilson as I Know Him* (Garden City, N.Y., 1921). Charles Seymour (ed.), *The Intimate Papers of Colonel House* (4 vols., Boston, 1926–1928), is an indispensable collateral personal source.

There are numerous technical studies of Wilson the statesman and diplomatist, but the following provide a good introduction to the political and diplomatic history of the Wilson era for the general reader: Arthur S. Link, *Wilson the Diplomatist* (Baltimore, 1963), and *Woodrow Wilson and the Progressive Era* (New York, 1963); William Diamond, *The Economic Thought of Woodrow Wilson* (Baltimore, 1943); Earl Latham (ed.), *The Philosophy and Policies of Woodrow Wilson* (Chicago, 1958); Wesley M. Baghy, *The Road to Normalcy, the Presidential Campaign and Election of 1920* (Baltimore, 1962); Thomas A. Bailey, *Woodrow Wilson and the Lost Peace* (New York, 1944), and *Woodrow Wilson and the Great Betrayal* (New York, 1945); Ray S. Baker, *Woodrow Wilson and World Settlement* (3 vols., Garden City, N.Y., 1922); Paul Birdsall, *Versailles Twenty Years After* (New York, 1941); and Edward M. House and Charles Seymour (eds.), *What Really Happened at Paris* (New York, 1921).

The only bibliography—*Woodrow Wilson: A Selected Bibliography*, by Laura S. Turnbull (Princeton, N.J., 1948)—is now somewhat dated.

Contributors

RAY STANNARD BAKER (1870–1946) began his long and varied career as one of the leading muckrakers for *McClure's* at the turn of the century. An editor of the *American Magazine* from 1906 to 1915, Baker was selected by President Wilson to direct the Press Bureau at the Paris Peace Conference. Baker received a Pulitzer Prize in 1940 for his eight-volume biographical study, *Woodrow Wilson: Life and Letters.*

SAMUEL G. BLYTHE (1868–1947) was chief Washington correspondent for the *New York World* from 1900 to 1907 and a staff writer for the *Saturday Evening Post* during the Wilson administration. A distinguished and respected journalist, Blythe was also the author of many books.

FRANK I. COBB (1869–1923) was chief editorial writer for the *Detroit Evening News* before becoming confidential adviser to Joseph Pulitzer in 1903. Upon Pulitzer's death in 1911, Cobb became editor-in-chief of the *New York World.* Cobb, through the editorial pages of the *World,* supported Wilson's bid for the Democratic nomination in 1912, thereby earning Wilson's gratitude and friendship.

CARY T. GRAYSON (1878–1938) was a naval surgeon on the Presidential yacht *Mayflower* during the Roosevelt and Taft administrations before becoming personal physician to President Wilson. He attended Wilson until Wilson's death in 1924.

WILLIAM BAYARD HALE (1869–1924) was one of the foremost journalists of the Wilsonian era and a Special Agent for President Wilson in Mexico and Central America. Later embittered by American participation in the First World War, Hale wrote *The Story of a Style* (1920), highly critical of Wilson.

BURTON J. HENDRICK (1870–1949) began his career in journalism with the New York *Evening Post* and *McClure's* magazine. He later became an editor of *World's Work*. He was the author of many books, two of which received a Pulitzer Prize—*The Life and Letters of Walter H. Page* (3 vols., 1922–1925) and *The Training of an American* (1928).

JAMES KERNEY (1873–1934), the self-educated son of Irish immigrants (he was one of nineteen children), held positions on various newspapers in New Jersey before becoming editor and part owner of the *Trenton Times* in 1903. Initially opposed to Wilson's candidacy for Governor in 1910, Kerney later swung his support to the Democratic nominee in the battle against bossism. Kerney was Director of the American Committee on Public Information in Paris during the First World War.

WILLIAM STARR MYERS (1877–1956) was Assistant Professor and Preceptor in History and Politics at Princeton from 1906 to 1918 and Professor of Politics from 1918 to 1943. He was a frequent contributor to newspapers and journals of opinion.

HERBERT G. NICHOLAS (1911–   ) is Nuffield Reader in the Comparative Study of Institutions at Oxford University and a Fellow of New College. A scholar of American history, he delivered the Shaw lectures in diplomatic history at The Johns Hopkins University in 1961 (published in 1963 as *Britain and the U.S.A.*).

ARCHIBALD W. PATTERSON (1858–1940), a fellow student with Wilson at the University of Virginia, practiced law in Richmond for many years.

BLISS PERRY (1860–1954), a distinguished scholar and teacher, taught at Princeton from 1893 to 1900. Later a Professor of English literature at Harvard, he was the author of numerous books and articles and an authority on Emerson.

CARL F. PRICE (1881–1948) was graduated from Wesleyan in 1902. He was best known as a composer of more than two hundred hymns and various cantatas.

CHARLES SEYMOUR (1885–1963) rose from Instructor in History at Yale in 1911 to President of the University in 1937. After serving as Chief of the Austro-Hungarian Division of the American Commission to Negotiate Peace, Seymour returned to Yale after the war to edit *The Intimate Papers of Colonel House* and to write several books on the diplomacy of the wartime period.

ARTHUR S. LINK, Edwards Professor of American History at Princeton University and Editor of *The Papers of Woodrow Wilson,* received his doctorate in history from the University of North Carolina in 1945. He has also taught at North Carolina State University, the University of North Carolina, and Northwestern University. He was the Harmsworth Professor of American History at Oxford University in 1958–1959 and Albert Shaw Lecturer at The Johns Hopkins University in 1956. His major published works are five volumes in a biography of Woodrow Wilson, two of which received Bancroft Prizes; a textbook in recent American History, *American Epoch;* and the volumes of *The Papers of Woodrow Wilson,* edited with associates at Princeton, three of which have appeared to date.

✪

AÏDA DIPACE DONALD, General Editor of the American Profiles series, holds degrees from Barnard and Columbia, where she taught American history, and a doctorate from the University of Rochester. Mrs. Donald has been awarded A.A.U.W. and Fulbright fellowships and has edited *John F. Kennedy and the New Frontier.* She is also co-editor of the *Diary of Charles Francis Adams.*